# HOW TO MANAGE
# COMMUNICATION
# PROBLEMS
## IN YOUNG CHILDREN

Second Edition
Edited by

Myra Kersner and Jannet A. Wright

**David Fulton Publishers**
London

David Fulton Publishers Ltd
2 Barbon Close, London WC1N 3JX

First published in Great Britain by
Winslow Press, 1993
Second Edition published in Great Britain by
David Fulton Publishers 1996

*British Library Cataloguing in Publication Data*

A catalogue record for this book is available from the British Library

ISBN 1-85346-414-7

Typeset by The Harrington Consultancy Ltd London N1
Printed in Great Britain by the Cromwell Press Ltd, Melksham

# HOW TO MANAGE
# COMMUNICATION

PROBLEMS
LEARNING
SUPIN YOUNG CHILDREN

City College
NORWICH

# Contents

# Acknowledgements

We would like to thank Gene Mahon for kindly providing us with the illustrations for Chapter 3.

We would also like to thank Ann Locke for her contribution to the Living Language section featured in Chapter 8 'Language Programmes' and Rachel Montgomery for her contribution to Chapter 7.

# Contributors

**Carolyn Bruce** is a lecturer in the Department of Human Communication Science at University College, London. As a speech and language therapist she has worked extensively with young children.

**Renée Byrne** is a specialist speech and language therapist working with people who stammer and is the author of *Let's Talk about Stammering.* She is also the adviser to the British Stammering Association.

**Myra Kersner** is a lecturer in the Department of Human Communication Science at University College, London. She was responsible for running speech and language courses for nursery nurses, teachers and educational psychologists. She has worked as a speech and language therapist in Yorkshire, London, and Toronto, Canada.

**Merle Mahon** is a lecturer in the Department of Human Communication Science at University College, London. She is qualified as a Speech Pathologist-Audiologist and holds an Advanced Clinical Skills Diploma of the College of Speech and Language Therapists in Speech Therapy with Deaf People.

**Carol Miller** is a senior lecturer in the School of Education, the University of Birmingham. She was formerly the Director of Studies at Cardiff School of Speech Therapy, where part of her work was in a Social Services family centre, helping young children and their parents.

**Magdalene Moorey** is a Senior Specialist Speech Language Therapist in south London. One of her areas of clinical interest is hearing impairment. She holds the Advanced Clinical Skills Diploma of the College of Speech and Language Therapists in Speech Therapy with Deaf People.

**Rosemarie MorganBarry** is a speech and language therapist who specialises in working with children with motor and structural speech disorders. She also works as a freelance lecturer.

**Alison Wintgens** is a speech and language therapist, with extensive experience in working with children with a range of special needs. She also lectures in this area. Her current post is in the Department of Child Psychiatry at St. George's Hospital, London.

**Sandy Winyard** has a qualification in psychology and speech and language therapy. She has lectured extensively on courses for nursery nurses and teachers in the area of speech and language development.

**Jannet A. Wright** is a senior lecturer in the Department of Human Communication Science at University College, London. She is a speech and language therapist who has specialised in working with children who have severe speech and language problems. She is responsible for organising speech and language courses for nursery nurses, teachers and educational psychologists.

# *Introduction*

For several years the Continuing Education Department of The National Hospital's College of Speech Sciences (now the Department of Human Communication Science, University College, London) organised courses to meet the needs of professionals who wanted to understand the specific difficulties and special communication needs of children in their care. These courses, run by speech and language therapists, included lectures and workshops on how to recognise particular problems, and offered suggestions for how to help when problems arise.

There were, however, many people who wanted to improve their knowledge and learn more about children's difficulties with communication, without attending courses. They wanted a book to read which did not assume prior specialist knowledge.

It was thus that the idea of the first edition of this book, published in 1993, was born. It was a book which covered much of the same content as the courses, which also explored other issues of particular interest to those working with young communication disordered children.

Many of those who taught on the original courses were invited to contribute to the book, as well as other specialist speech and language therapists who had specific expertise and experience with such children.

Learning to talk is something which most children do naturally and without fuss; helping children to communicate and develop speech and language is something which most adults do spontaneously and without thought. There is no need for us to understand this process, the child's role or the adult's role; no reason to know why, or how, speech and language develop – that is, until something goes wrong. It is not until we come across children who are experiencing difficulties, and are not learning to talk, easily and routinely, that we go in search of knowledge. Then we urgently try to find out more about speech and language development, try to discover what has gone wrong, and how we might be able to help put it right.

It is not only parents of young children who might find themselves in this situation. Nursery nurses, care officers, welfare or classroom assistants, as well as nursery or mainstream infant teachers, may find that they are working with children with speech, language and communication difficulties, who seem to have no other major problems, and they too welcome information regarding disorders of communication.

The aim of the book was to offer some insight and understanding of some of these difficulties: to indicate what signs to look out for; offer some interpretation of what these signs might mean; and suggest how best to help, and where and how to seek expert advice. Much of the text of the first edition is still valid, although in this second edition we have made additions and alterations to reflect new developments and current practice.

We hope that this second edition will prove to be a useful text for our colleagues and fellow professionals, and that it may also be helpful for those who are contemplating a career working with young children, by highlighting some of the problems which they will encounter. In addition we hope that it may be a source book for parents helping them to understand more fully their children's difficulties, and thus enabling us all to work together for the benefit of the children in our care.

Myra Kersner, Jannet A. Wright

# CHAPTER 1

# How to Manage Communication Problems in Young Children

## Myra Kersner

SPEECH, LANGUAGE and COMMUNICATION are words which most of us use, comfortably and often, taking for granted that we understand their meaning according to different contexts, and, when they are used by speech and language therapists in a professional context, they take on a specific meaning. This book has been written by speech and language therapists, and, throughout the text of the following chapters, these three words are referred to in their technical sense, in terms of the developing child. It is important therefore that they should be clearly defined at the outset, and that the relationship between them in this context be explained. (See Figure 1.1).

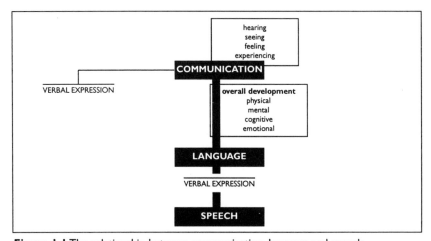

**Figure 1.1** The relationship between communication, language and speech

Figure 1.1 illustrates in summary how communication develops as the new born baby sees, hears and begins to experience the world. Initially the baby communicates using **nonverbal expression** such as crying, laughing or cooing. As the child begins to develop physically, cognitively and emotionally, so the understanding of language develops. This language may then be communicated using **Verbal Expression** or **Speech**. (This is more fully developed in Chapter 2).

## Communication

Communication is about receiving and expressing messages. It is generally defined in terms of social interaction – people talking to each other. However, it is more than that. Communication may occur without people talking; for instance, newborn children communicate long before language or speech have developed, and adults in turn communicate with them (see Chapter 2).

From the first day of life, babies receive communication from others, albeit passively, as they begin to see, hear and experience the world around them. When they are held close by a caring adult, when they hear words of comfort, or even angry tones, or when they are merely taking part in the feeding process, they are receiving communication from others.

At the same time, babies are able to communicate actively, and express themselves, because, from the day they are born, they are able to tell us when they are wet, hungry or uncomfortable.

There are three basic elements required for expressive communication: **intention, the means, a receiver**.

*Intention:* this refers to the intention to convey a message, for example babies have the intention when they have the need, almost from the moment of birth, to convey a message expressing their discomfort.

*The means:* this is the means by which that message may be conveyed. In young babies for example, the means to express their discomfort is by crying.

*A receiver:* this refers to the person who is required to 'pick up' and respond to the message once it has been sent. With young babies it is usually the parent or carer who hears them crying and is ready to react and respond.

These three elements of communication are usually in place at birth, and it is from this cycle that early **communication patterns** are set, (see Figure 1.2).

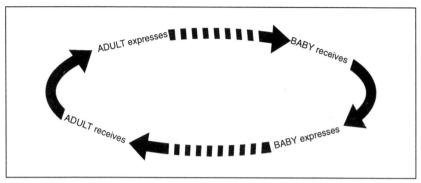

**Figure 1.2** Communication patterns

As Figure 1.2 illustrates, the baby expresses discomfort by crying; the adult carer receives that message and responds, perhaps with soothing words or noises; the baby hears these noises and responds, perhaps with a modified type of expression such as a whimper, or a comfort noise. It is also important to notice that when an adult receives the baby's first message s/he will probably respond, in addition, with an action, such as feeding the baby, or changing its nappy. This action will reinforce the baby's intention to communicate, because the baby will realise that its attempts to communicate are rewarded by adults' actions.

At first babies are only able to communicate their feelings of discomfort, by crying, but gradually they begin to signal: 'I am happy; I am comfortable,' by cooing, gurgling, or smiling, and the cycle once again is reinforced. Normally, this repertoire of pre-language, nonverbal forms of expression, increases as children develop more understanding of language, until finally, they are ready to speak (see Chapter 2).

## Language

Although communication begins at birth, language does not develop until the child begins to grow and mature, absorbing sensory experiences from the outside world. Language is extremely complex, although, once acquired, we use it extensively and automatically (Syder, 1992). The very young baby, however, 'is motivated to be a good communicator, so that by the time language comes "on line" at around the first birthday, most of the basic capacity to use it has already developed' (Law, 1992, p18).

Language is a form of shorthand which is used as a means of classifying and ordering the world. Various symbols are used to represent objects, situations, and the everyday occurrences of life. These symbols are the spoken or written words which, over generations, have evolved (and continue to evolve) into an agreed and accepted system of symbols – a particular language. In our case this is English, a system of symbols governed by over 1000 grammatical rules (Crystal, 1986) all of which are accepted and recognised both in this country and by many people throughout the world. Adults may be expected to have about 50,000 different words which they are able to use, and they will often understand and recognise up to twice that number (Crystal, 1986).

As young children are helped to understand the symbols of their own language (see Chapter 2), gradually they are able to use that language to express their own messages and to improve their communication. It is surprising to realise how many words may be used even by young children. A study cited in Crystal, 1986, shows that at seventeen months one child was able to use 1860 different types of words. These included nouns, naming people and different categories of objects; verbs, describing a variety of actions; descriptive words referring to location, and words such as 'more' and 'again'.

The use of language means that a greater variety of messages may be communicated to larger numbers of people. Language allows messages to be more precisely expressed, so that they will be understood by more people. For example, the mother of a fifteen month old boy may understand that when he says: 'er do do' and points his finger, he means, 'There's a bus over there', but she may be the only person who understands this. However, anyone who understands English will know what he means once he is able to say the words: 'Look, there's a bus'. By the time the child is five, he may be expected to use over 2400 different types of words (Crystal, 1986).

Language may be expressed in a variety of ways (see below). Most commonly however, it is expressed through words which are spoken out loud.

## Speech

Speech may be thought of as verbal expression, and it is the mechanism by which most people communicate. Speech requires the use of the voice to make sounds. These sounds are then formed and shaped by the tongue, lips, teeth and palate to make the 20 vowel sounds and 24 consonant sounds of English, which are then combined in over 300 different ways to form English words (Crystal, 1986). When these words are heard and recognised by others, they are responded to with other words; thus the links between speech, language and communication are formed and the relationship completed. How this relationship develops is explained in detail in the next chapter.

## Other ways of expressing language

There are other ways in which language may be expressed nonverbally. As Figure 1.3 shows, as well as using speech, language may be expressed using two other forms of nonverbal expression: **Non-vocal Expression,** and **Body Language**.

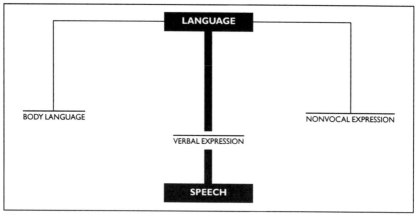

**Figure 1.3** Verbal and Nonverbal Expression

### Non-vocal expression

There are several forms of non-vocal expression. One commonly used way to express the words of language is to make them into written symbols (letters), and to write them down and read them. Reading and writing as a form of expression is usually learned after speech has developed, when children go to school.

There are some children however, who understand language, but whose speech does not develop properly; they have to learn to express their language in other ways. This may occur with children who have hearing problems, or with some of those who have learning difficulties; it may be that they have a physical handicap, such as cerebral palsy, or they may have a specific problem affecting the speech organs such as paralysis or a degenerative disease.

In such cases these children may be taught an alternative system of communication such as a sign language (British Sign Language, Paget Gorman Sign System, or Makaton – see Appendix); a symbol system where they point to pictures, words or specific symbols (Rebus, Makaton Symbols, or Blissymbolics – see Appendix), or they may use written words if they are able to read and write.

In some cases a technical aid such as a specially adapted electronic typewriter, or a synthesised voice, may provide a special alternative to speech.

## Body Language

Body language is yet another example of nonverbal expression. These messages, however, which may be sent either consciously or unconsciously, are usually used in addition to the spoken word. This form of nonverbal expression amplifies speech, giving it another dimension, sometimes even another meaning.

An example of body language is making eye contact, or alternatively, avoiding someone's gaze. This gives unspoken messages about the level of shyness, awkwardness, embarrassment or confidence which one may be feeling during a particular interaction.

Stance gives another message. The arms akimbo position of fists on the waist with the elbows pointing outwards is often considered to look aggressive, whereas the arms folded across the chest may be interpreted as defensive.

Gestures may help to emphasise a spoken message, such as wagging a finger while telling someone off. Gestures may even replace the spoken word, such as when pointing, or shrugging the shoulders.

Different facial expressions also give additional messages. Smiling or frowning may quickly convey an accurate message regarding feelings, which may help to underline the words of the message.

However, facial expressions may also be used to convey 'a mixed message.' This may occur for example when the speaker uses an angry voice which is belied by a twinkle of the eye; or when seemingly harmless words are combined with a sarcastic lifting of the eyebrows. Such nonverbal messages play an important role in communication.

## Difficulties with communication

Sometimes, however, the ideal relationship between communication, speech and language is not achieved. The links are not made and communication, at some level, breaks down. In such instances, children may be said to have a 'communication disorder' which is an 'umbrella term' covering a wide range of difficulties concerning speech, language and communication (Syder 1992). Crystal (1984) suggested that around 10 per cent of all pre-school and school aged children have speech and language problems, and Webster (1988) says that as many as 5 per cent of children enter school with some of these difficulties. It would therefore seem to be important for nursery nurses, teachers and careworkers to ensure that they have an understanding of children's speech and language problems. Indeed, because of the opportunities which are now available for more children with special educational needs to enter mainstream schools, as well as the introduction of the National Curriculum, Miller (1991) argues that more teachers will require more knowledge and skills in the management of children with speech and language difficulties. This view is supported by the findings of a study in 1989 by the Association for All Speech Impaired Children (AFASIC).

The relationship between communication, language and speech is a complex one and the ability to communicate is dependent on the social and emotional as well as the physical environment (Syder, 1992). It is therefore possible that it could break down at any stage during a child's development. The effect this would have on the young child would depend at which level of this relationship the breakdown occurred.

For example, if something went wrong during the early stages of development, before the patterns of communication were fully established, this could result in the child having difficulties in the subsequent development of language, and later, speech. If, conversely, there were for example a physical problem affecting the organs of speech, this would not necessarily affect language development or the establishment of communication patterns.

## Describing children's speech and language

Which terms to use to describe children's abnormal speech and language development is often a point for discussion among speech and language therapists. For example, there is debate, but not always agreement, regarding the use of terms such as 'disordered', and 'delayed', when should one be used, when the other? This text does not attempt to make such distinctions. In the following chapters, such words as 'delayed; disordered; difficulties; problems; impairment' are used interchangeably.

However, it is always advisable to discuss such terms with your speech and language therapist colleagues, to ensure that they are being used in the same descriptive way by all those working together with any particular child.

Whilst it may not be important to differentiate the terminology, it is important to be able to recognise children who have problems; to be able to classify broadly the area in which they (the children) are having the most difficulty – is it with language? with speech? or with basic patterns of communication? – and know how to begin to help. If children are not given such help at the appropriate time the overall effect may be that their communicative skills, 'may be learned late, incorrectly, or not at all,' (Weiss and Lilleywhite, 1981).

## The population of children

The children described in this book are, in the main, the kind of children who may be found in an ordinary nursery or a mainstream classroom. They may seem to be 'normal' in many ways and yet they are children who are obviously experiencing some difficulties with speech/ language/communication. These are the children who are often in danger of being overlooked, if their particular difficulty is not understood. There are several reasons which might account for their speech and language difficulties, some of which will be dealt with in the following chapters. These include: hearing difficulties; speech and language problems; emotional and behavioural problems, and stammering.

### Hearing difficulties

The ability to hear is normally present at least from the moment of birth. If there are difficulties with this basic, fundamental sensory system, it can be seen from Figure 1.1 how the entire communication system and the development of language and speech may be affected subsequently to some degree. Weiss and Lilleywhite (1981), report that about 1 in 20 children may enter school with a hearing handicap, because carers have not been able to recognise the problem, or have not known what to do about it if a loss was suspected. Details of the development of the auditory system and how hearing impairment may affect the young child are described in Chapter 3.

### Speech and language problems

Although diagnosis of specific syndromes and disorders requires the specialist knowledge of a speech and language therapist, nursery nurses, teachers and careworkers are often able to recognise and describe children's communication disorders. Weiss, Lilleywhite and Gordon, (1980) report that in young children with speech and language difficulties, 17 per cent of these problems are related to language, and 75 per cent related to articulation. There is a description and discussion in Chapter 4 of how to recognise and distinguish some of these difficulties. For example, how to recognise problems in the communication patterns described in Figure 1.2; how to recognise difficulties with understanding language; and how to recognise some expressive language and articulation difficulties, such as the development of certain sounds.

## Stammering

Stammering is a specific problem affecting the speech and language of people of all ages. Weiss et al (1980) say that such difficulties constitute 3 per cent of all speech and language disorders in young children. Although fewer children are affected by stammering than by other disorders, as described above, stammering may sometimes prove more difficult to manage than some articulation problems. Stammering affects verbal expression, the speech and language output, which may sound as if it were 'broken up' and not fluent. The problems which arise with children who stammer, and how they may be helped, are dealt with in Chapter 5.

## Emotional and behavioural difficulties

Although emotional difficulties may arise as a result of speech and language disorders, and the resultant frustration of having an impaired communication system, it can be seen from Figure 1.1 that emotional development plays an important role in the development of the child as a whole, and particularly in the development of language speech. Some emotional and behavioural difficulties may also be the cause of communication and/or language difficulties. This is discussed more fully in Chapter 6.

# The involvement of the speech and language therapist

A survey of Health Authorities in the UK by VOCAL, in 1987, revealed that staffing ratios of therapists to children were not at recommended levels. However, wherever possible it is best to seek the advice of a speech and language therapist to discuss the ways in which to help any child with a communication difficulty, even if s/he is not able to see the child regularly. The role of the speech and language therapist is not always understood and Chapter 7 has been included in order to explain this role as well as where to find the local speech and language therapist, the relationship of the speech and language therapist to other professionals, and how children may be referred.

## How can you help?

The development of language and speech is an intrinsic and integral part of the development of the child as a whole, and there are many ways in which children can be helped if they are experiencing difficulties with this aspect of their development. Chapter 8 contains suggestions for enhancing language development by discussing formal language 'programmes'. These have been specifically devised, and several may appear in published form, which may be of use in the classroom or nursery. However, there are many games and activities, which are useful for such children and teachers could include as part of their regular busy classroom schedule; many such activities which could become part of a nursery nurse's routine. Ideas and suggestions for the inclusion of these informal activities are given in Chapter 9.

## Working with parents

Wherever possible, professionals should not work in isolation with children who have problems, that is, without consultation and reference to the home. It is acknowledged that parents are often among the first to recognise that something is wrong with their child; it is therefore important for them to be included in the helping process, whenever possible. How professionals may approach and facilitate this aspect of their work is discussed in the final chapter.

There are, of course, many other groups of children who have speech and language difficulties who are not specifically referred to in this book. Mostly these are children who have communication disorders as a result of other disabilities such as cerebral palsy, or other physical handicaps; severe or mild learning difficulties, or have been diagnosed as autistic. Many of these children have a multiple combination of problems and need specific specialist help which may be beyond the scope of the routine nursery or classroom schedule. Perhaps they will be the subject of another book.

# CHAPTER 2

# *The Development of Communication – Speech and Language Acquisition*

## Sandy Winyard

The process of communicating starts from birth, and, as has been shown in Chapter 1, the development of communication into language and speech begins as the new born baby draws its first breath.

Communication is an **interactive process**; that means, more than one person is involved. Even from birth it is something that does not occur alone, it is dependent on other factors, like people and events. This can be illustrated by thinking about any conversation. What one person says is dependent on what the other person says; on their reactions to the first person's communication.

Communication is both verbal and non verbal. The verbal part of the communication is the words that are spoken. The nonverbal part consists of facial expression, such as smiling, frowning, questioning; eye contact; and gestures, such as beckoning, pointing, or waving. Our body language also provides nonverbal information for the listener. For example, slouching and turning away from someone indicates disinterest and boredom, while sitting up straight and turning towards someone indicates interest and attention. Normally, communication requires both verbal and nonverbal skills and it is important to remember that much information is conveyed by both methods.

## Language development

Language can be divided into **expression** and **comprehension**. Expression – is what children say or do that conveys what they want to communicate. Comprehension – is what children understand from verbal messages, when they are spoken to, and what they understand from what is conveyed in a nonverbal way by gestures and/or body language.

Language can be described by breaking it down into several parts.

## Sounds

The sounds in spoken English do not match the letters of the alphabet. For example:

- the letter 'a' is pronounced or sounded differently in the words: 'pan'; 'pane'; 'park';
- the 'sh' sound in words like 'shop' and 'shape' is said as one sound but it is written with two letters from the alphabet;
- 'cat' is written with three letters and has three sounds c-a-t, but 'sharp' has five letters and three sounds sh-ar-p.

When children are learning to talk, it is the sounds that are learnt, not the letters. It is these sounds with which they sometimes have problems. (See Chapter 4)

## Content

This is the words or **vocabulary** which make up the meaning of a message; that is, what children want to convey. Children may sometimes try to convey the same message as an adult, but the way that they say it may sound different. Child language is different from adult language. It is not incorrect or wrong, rather it is developing.

Some children may pronounce the words incorrectly. For example, they may confuse some sounds in words so that they say 'tat' instead of 'cat', or 'gog' instead of 'dog'.

Their sentences may be incomplete. For example: 'Daddy sock,' may mean 'Daddy I want my sock,' or 'This is Daddy's sock.'

The order of the words may be incorrect. For example, a child may say, 'Go car me,' instead of, 'Me go car,' meaning 'I want to go in the car.'

However, despite sounding different, the message may still be clear to the listener because **contextual clues** may be given; that is, information which will help the understanding of the message. This may come from the general situation, or from previous knowledge and information which is known to the two people who are communicating.

For example, Tom asks his mother: 'Where loon?' What he means is, 'Where is the balloon?'

His mother's interpretation of this is dependent on her knowledge of his language and her knowledge of her child and his environment. His mother may know that he has been playing with the balloon, or that he has called it a 'loon' previously, or she may have been told about it by someone who has seen the balloon game. Because she has this information, the mother can understand what Tom is saying.

## *Grammar*

This refers to the rules of language. The words which express ideas, give information and convey feelings are not put together in a haphazard way. They are organised into structured sentences according to grammatical rules. These rules of language are sometimes referred to as **syntax**.

For example, when describing the size and colour of an object in English, size always comes before the colour. Thus we say a 'big, blue ball', not a 'blue, big ball'.

In summary: language comprises sounds, which combine to make words, which combine to make sentences.

## *Use*

This is sometimes known as **pragmatics**. This refers to the way language, both verbal and nonverbal, is used.

For example, children talk to their playmates in a different way than they talk to their teachers.

## *Intonation*

This means the rising or falling sound patterns of speech, or the melody. It plays an important role in communication because it is this melody which is one of the first features of speech and language that children both understand and produce. The intonation carries much of the information about the content or meaning of the message.

In English, the intonation usually goes down at the end of a sentence. For example, if the sentence, 'We're going out,' is said as a statement, announcing the intention to go out, the voice will drop at the end. Try saying it.

The same sentence can be turned into a question by changing the intonation pattern. For a question, the intonation rises at the end. Now try saying, 'We're going out?' as a question. Can you hear the difference?

Young children rely on the information provided by intonation patterns to help them understand what is said, long before they understand the individual words in a sentence they hear.

In order to produce the melodies of intonation and to communicate verbally, we need to use our voices.

### Voice

When you open your mouth and a sound comes out – any sound from your throat – this is voice. Voice is produced when yelling, shouting, or speaking. The air which we breathe in is forced out of our lungs through our mouths and/or noses. This stream of air passes through the vocal cords or folds which are situated in the neck. Try putting a finger on your Adam's apple, the lump of cartilage on the front of your neck, the vocal cords or **larynx** are within this protuberance. Say 'bbb'. You will feel vibrations. This is because the vocal cords are vibrating as the air passes through them.

Children frequently use a loud voice, and at school they often shout and yell in the playground. It is possible for their voices to become hoarse because of excessive shouting; then they may need to be seen by a speech and language therapist who will help them use their voices less stridently.

The same can happen to adults, especially teachers who have to project their voices over a noisy classroom; they may strain their voices and become hoarse. They may even 'lose' their voice. If this happens, they too may need help from a speech and language therapist, or from a doctor, or an Ear, Nose and Throat Specialist (ENT).

## How do children learn language?

### Imitation

If asked how children learn language, a number of people would say, by imitation – they hear words and copy them. There is no doubt that some of the words children produce are imitated. For example, three year old Sam was overheard saying to his best friend, 'You can't have ice cream until you've eaten your dinner.' He used exactly the same words, as well as the voice and intonation pattern that his mother used to him a few days earlier. This is a clear example of imitation.

However, imitation cannot tell the whole story about how children learn to speak. Even allowing for the fact that children hear many different examples of language, from many different sources, such as at home, with friends and friends' families, in playgroup or school, or even local shops, imitation cannot account for the new and original ways in which children then produce and use language themselves.

If children learned to speak only by imitation we should expect children's speech to be the same as adults' speech. However, as we saw before, the language of the child is not a replica of the language of an adult – it is different. It seems to have its own patterns and to follow its own rules.

No matter how often you say, 'Daddy has just gone to work in the car,' children can only attempt to repeat such a sentence using the language which corresponds with the level or stage of their development. For example, in the case of two and a half year old Tom, his attempted repetition of this sentence was, 'Daddy go work car.'

Another way children's speech differs is that children do not indulge in 'babytalk' in the way many adults do. For example, how many children refer to their toes as, 'piggy wiggys'? or their breakfast of a boiled egg as an 'eggy weggy?'

Another argument against imitation is that, by adult standards, children's language is full of errors. For example, children talk about 'mouses' – they do not immediately imitate 'mice'. Similarly they use 'goed' instead of 'went' and 'badder' instead of 'worse'. This is quite normal – all children go through these stages while they are developing language. The rate at which they develop may vary, some take longer than others to progress through the stages of 'child language' to mature language structures.

## Innate ability

If imitation does not explain how language develops, then what is the explanation? How do children develop language? There are some researchers such as Chomsky (1959) who feel that children are born with an innate ability to produce language. The language they are exposed to in their environment, which they hear all around them, then triggers this inbuilt ability.

This theory certainly offers an explanation as to how children are able to learn a limited number of words and use them in combinations which they have obviously never heard before.

## Adult-child interaction and the development of language

Both of the previously mentioned theories about language development – imitation and innateness – focus on the child. They do not take into account the people who communicate, or interact with the child. A view which does take into account these people, and the children's interaction, is that suggested by Bruner (1975). His theory focuses on the person in conversation with the child, for example the mother. Bruner's theory tries to examine what she is saying to her child and how she responds to the child's efforts to communicate with her. This verbal interaction and the mother's contribution or **input** is now thought to be fundamental to the child's normal development of speech and language.

Viewed from the perspective of the child, language development in terms of adult:child interaction may be considered in two stages – pre-verbal and verbal.

### *Pre-verbal stage*

The pre-verbal stage covers the period from babies' first cries to the emergence of their first words. The adults' input during this stage is important because, initially, it is the way adults respond to the cries and physical actions of babies that gives those cries and actions meaning. A baby who wriggles, kicks and cries could be trying to communicate:

'I'm hungry';
'I'm uncomfortable and wet and want to be changed';
'I want to be picked up and made a fuss of'.

The adult interprets the meaning by responding to the baby's behaviour, for example by offering food, changing a dirty nappy, or picking up and cuddling the infant. The way the adult responds will influence the child's behaviour.

In this way children learn that some of their messages mean something to the adults around them, and that some of their messages are ignored and need to be altered before the adults will respond in the required way.

Of course, this can be a two-way process and sensitive adults learn from the babies' responses whether they have responded appropriately to the messages.

During this pre-verbal stage babies spend a great deal of time practising the sounds and melodies of speech. They will make noises, their mothers will often make the same noises back. This is one of the ways in which babies learn the **turn-taking skills** which are required for later stages in their language development when they need to learn to take turns, similarly, in verbal conversations.

### Listening and attention

In order to interact in this way young children have to be able to listen and pay attention, and, long before they can talk, they will listen and attend when an adult is talking. Listening and attending is more than just hearing, it is more than just being aware of noises and happenings all around; it involves actively concentrating on the noises in the environment. Babies demonstrate that they are really listening by focussing on the adult's face and stopping all activity while the adult is talking. When the adult stops talking they start to make noises and thrash around with their limbs as they 'take their turn' in the conversation.

By about nine months children realize that they can influence adult behaviour by using various communication strategies like gestures, vocalisations, or even by making eye contact. This may be considered to be intentional behaviour because children really want the particular message they are sending to be understood. They know what they are trying to communicate and are sending signals using the same combination of sounds, gestures or looks which in the past have achieved the answer they want from the adult.

For example, baby Wayne, at eleven months, knows that the sounds, 'erer' said with a certain intonation, together with a pointing gesture, always result in him getting a drink. Therefore he will reproduce it next time he wants a drink.

### Child-directed speech

When interacting with young babies, adults employ a different sort of communication style. This child-directed speech (or 'motherese' as it was sometimes known) tends to be simpler than the speech used when talking to an adult; and, while the sentences are correct in grammar and sounds, they tend to be short and simple in their construction. Speech is often slower, louder, and on a higher note; and words which the adult really wants the child to understand are emphasised by putting more stress on them. For example: 'Tom, go and get the ball, get *the ball.*'

### Vocal play

While building turn-taking skills with their mothers, babies still have time for practising their speech, by playing with sounds. They progress from crying and making basic sounds through happy cooing noises to vocal play. Vocal play is quite melodic and babies often bang toys in time with their vocalisations. This stage is reached at about four months.

For example, Jane was four months old when she began to produce a greater variety of sounds – vowel sounds like 'ah' and 'oo' and oh' and consonant sounds like 'g, k, m' became common. She produced one sound and then repeated it over and over again. She also produced trills and blew 'raspberries'. All of these are common features at this age, and are typical of vocal play.

### Babbling

At about six months the babbling stage begins. Most people are familiar with this and remember the long strings of 'babababababa' or 'dadadadada' which infants produce. As the baby continues to babble, the sounds become more varied and change within the string, so that strings like: 'madumadu' may be produced.

### Jargon

At about nine months the intonation patterns of speech are picked up more intensely and practised. Gradually the length of sounds children produce increases and they sound as if they are producing adult speech. In fact, they are not using real words, they are producing strings of sounds with intonation patterns they have learnt from adults. This is called jargon.

By the end of this phase, children are ready to enter the verbal stage. They have acquired many **functional communication skills**: they have learnt the conversational skills of turn-taking, listening and attending; they have practised using their voice, different intonation patterns and sounds; they have practised using some content, and getting their message across to their listener. They continue to practise these functional communication skills, by making their needs known, and manipulating their world by intentionally communicating. They have begun to realise the power of language and they have not yet said a word!

## Verbal stage

Into this nonverbal framework of sounds and intonation, the child, at about twelve to fifteen months, begins to insert words. The first words children say are usually the names of things that are in their personal world which are important to them. The first words might be, 'cup', 'bear', 'car', 'drink', names of the family, or pets. These words may not be pronounced perfectly; for example, cup might be 'cu' or drink might be 'dint' or 'dink'. However, by this stage, the word is always used to mean the same thing, showing that the child has attached meaning to it and is using it consistently to convey the same message.

## Generalisation

Sometimes children use the same word to mean a number of things that seem similar to them. So, the word 'dog', for a period in the child's development of language, might be used for all the four legged animals the child comes across, such as dogs, cats and horses.

A common example of this **generalisation** is the use of the word 'Daddy' or 'Mummy'. Once learnt, 'Daddy' may then be used for all men, and 'Mummy' for all women. A similar process may also happen with the name of the family pet. It is very common to hear a child calling everybody's cat 'Smokey' because that is the name of their own family's cat. Gradually children learn to refine these 'umbrella' terms or generalisations and learn, for example, that a cat is different from a dog. They also learn that their Daddy is called Daddy by them, but that other people may use first names, or surnames.

### The 'two-word' stage

A little later in their development – from approximately two years upwards – children begin to put two words together. These two word phrases or sentences are the beginnings of real grammar and may represent a number of different functions like statements, requests and questions.

For example:

- 'Car gone,' is a statement meaning, 'The car has gone.'
- 'Mummy biscuit?' is a request meaning, 'Mummy, please may I have a biscuit.'
- 'Where train?' – spoken with a rising inflection – is a question meaning, 'Where is the train?' or, 'Where has the train gone?'

These are examples of how children are able to get their message across, successfully, to their listeners using a restricted and immature grammar or rule system, and knowing only a small number of words.

How the listener interprets the meaning of the child's language is important. For example, when two year old Samantha says a phrase like 'Mummy shoe' she might mean:

'Mummy, where's my shoe?' (a question);
or, 'Mummy, where's your shoe?' (a question);
or, 'Mummy, here's your shoe' (a statement);
or, 'Mummy, here's my shoe' (a statement).

The intonation pattern will reveal whether she meant the words to be a question or a statement. But, whether she meant it to refer to her Mother's shoe or to her own shoe will be revealed by contextual clues, such as the general situation, or by other language that has been used before or after the phrase in question.

A child may want to convey a number of different messages by using the same two words, and it is only by understanding the situation and listening to the intonation pattern that the listener can make the correct interpretation. This illustrates how the listener, the person with whom the child is communicating, helps the child to expand his/her language skills. The listener does this by understanding the message the child is trying to communicate as well as by using other clues such as the intonation pattern, the environment they are in, and any gestures which the child may use to help communication. The listener shows that they have understood by responding appropriately.

### Acknowledging, reinforcing, modelling and expanding

Adults help children to develop their language skills by acknowledging that they have said something, reinforcing what they have said and modelling a correct or mature response. They may also expand what children have said, providing more information about the subject, so that children's vocabulary and knowledge of the language grows.

For example, Katherine aged two and a half and her mother are out shopping in the High Street one day. Katherine suddenly says: 'Mummy, bu', pointing at the bus. Her mother replies appropriately: 'Yes, it's a bus' (reinforcing and modelling). She then expands: 'A big, red bus with people on. We could go on a bus to see granny tomorrow. Would you like that?'

Katherine's mother has provided acknowledgement, by saying, 'Yes.' She has reinforced and provided the correct model, by repeating what Katherine has said, but using the adult form, 'bus' instead of 'bu'; and she has expanded what Katherine said by telling her more about it. This will encourage Katherine to keep the conversation going, because her mother showed interest in what she was talking about. Her mother did not introduce a new subject of her own choosing; she followed Katherine's lead by talking about her choice of subject. If she is responded to in this way, Katherine should feel good about communicating and hopefully will continue to do it, learning all the time.

These strategies can be particularly useful if children are having difficulty learning to talk. Then the adults around them have to become aware of strategies which they may have used previously, unconsciously, and try to use them intentionally in order to encourage language development.

If you think about how you communicate with children, you probably do this quite naturally most of the time. Try and be aware of the messages you are giving to the children you talk to. Are you encouraging, like Katherine's mother in the example above? Or could your messages sound discouraging? This could be conveyed for example, by not acknowledging what the child has said, or by changing the subject to one of your own choice.

The work of people such as Gordon Wells (1985) suggests that children practise language skills with children of their own age, but learn language from people who are older and are more sophisticated, and who are skilled language users themselves. Older children and adults are therefore able to reinforce and expand vocabulary, language structure and general experience.

## Concept development

At the same time as language is developing, young children are developing concepts. These help them to put some order into their world and to understand the world around them. Concept development may be reflected in their use of language, although the stages of development of concepts and language do not always coincide.

### *Possession*

Once the idea of possession creeps into the child's language, the word 'mine' may be used a great deal, although not always appropriately, such as in 'Mine teddy', 'Mine cup'. The word 'yours' may be used, but again, probably inappropriately, because the concept of sharing one's possessions with someone else is not yet understood.

### *Position*

Similarly, when children begin to use words which indicate position, for example: 'in; on; under', the ability to use such words correctly is linked to their intellectual development. Children will begin to use the words in phrases such as 'doll in chair', 'carrot on table' long before they have understood that 'in; on; under' refer to a specific position.

### Size, shape colour

The words indicating the size, shape or colour of an object may be used at first in imitation, without any real understanding of what they mean. As children begin to understand the concepts of size and shape, they may begin to use the words appropriately, for example: 'Dat big cup', 'My big bed'. Between their third and fourth birthday they will begin to recognise and name colours as in: 'Where yellow ball?'

The understanding and use of position words and vocabulary to describe size and colour gives children a more precise grasp of language. When asking for a special cup from the top shelf in the kitchen, they can now say, 'Red one,' which is much quicker and more efficient than saying, 'Dat one,' and pointing. Although previously the message would have been understood, it might have taken longer, depending on the number of choices, to convey the same information. Children quickly learn how useful it is to be able to be more precise with language, and may well practise their new skills by demanding all sorts of things.

Adults also enjoy children's growing language skills as it means they no longer have to spend as much time working out the meaning of what children are saying. Communication is quicker and more fun, with new vocabulary being used all the time. As children take a greater part in doing things in the home and actually experience tasks like washing up, hoovering, making the beds and fixing broken objects they will talk about them at the same time. This gives them the best possible experience of language at its most meaningful.

## The development of grammatical structure

By the third year, children are quite sophisticated language users, able to make statements and describe things, ask questions and claim possession of things appropriately. The third year is often thought of as being the one when most linguistic progress occurs, although to the adult listener the child's speech is full of grammatical errors. For example, word endings are often incorrect.

# Tenses

When trying to form the past tense of a verb, children work out that there is a rule about adding '-ed' to some words, when talking about what they did yesterday. They will then over-generalise this new rule, adding '-ed' to all verbs, producing words like:

- 'I goed or wented' instead of 'I went';
- 'I runned' instead of 'I ran';
- 'I eated' instead of 'I ate'.

This is because they have learnt the rule that applies in English to regular verbs such as, 'walk, jump, want.' The past tense of the verb is formed by adding '-ed'. Children therefore often apply this rule to all verbs. Unfortunately, in English, there are many irregular verbs where this rule does not apply, such as sleep (slept), come (came), and those given above.

The future tense which is regularly formed by adding 'will' as in: 'I will come', 'I will jump' does not appear in their speech until children develop their concept of future time.

## *Plurals*

The same mistakes will occur as with past tenses, when children need to form the plural of nouns. They learn the regular rule that if they are referring to more than one object, they need to add an 's' such as, 'bed/beds.'

However, this does not work for irregular nouns like mouse (mice), sheep (sheep), foot (feet). In an attempt to apply the newly learnt rule children will often produce the words 'mouses; sheeps, and feets.' Gradually they learn the correct form. This is partly achieved by adults responding in the way previously described; that is, giving the correct and accepted model of the word, while reinforcing the use of the meaning.

## *Questions*

In the early stages of language development, questions are asked using a rising intonation pattern. For example, 'Me going out?'; 'Daddy go work?' Then, children learn that specific question words such as 'Where? What? Why? When How' get both adult attention and information, and they begin to use these words often. Such questions can be a cause of great embarrassment to adults, as they are not always used in the appropriate time and place. This is a great delight to children, often encouraging them to do it again. This is demonstrated in the following example:

On a crowded bus, Lucy aged three asks, in a loud voice about the young girl sitting two seats in front: 'Mummy, why has that lady got pink hair?' Observing the reaction both from her mother and everyone else on the bus, Lucy is encouraged to repeat it. The response, reaction and information gained from using question words means that children will use them frequently.

The third year is often described as the 'why' stage.

### Word order

Children are learning and absorbing so much new information about their environment and language, that they sometimes get their words in the wrong order. For example, saying sentences like: 'They looked at very funny faces with each other,' instead of, 'They looked at each other with very funny faces.' It is usually when children are trying out new constructions that they make errors. However, even when making errors, children usually succeed in getting their message across correctly.

As children begin to have more to say, they want to talk in longer more complex sentences to get their ideas across. At first they cope with this by linking several short sentences together using the word 'and'.

For example: 'And we're going there and teddy and I want dolly and that doll and that one and Rupert Bear.'

Gradually other words, such as 'like; but; because; so; or,' are used. They enable children to use complex sentences containing more than one idea, linking the ideas together.

For example: 'Can we go to the beach, because I want to swim?' or 'I want to go out, but it's raining.'

## Conclusion

At this stage, the sounds of the words may still not be pronounced correctly, but this does not matter as long as the message is being received successfully. The practice children are getting when talking and using language helps them to make refinements to their sound system.

Children continue to make grammatical errors until ten years or sometimes even later (Chomsky, 1969). For example, an eleven year old girl said: 'When we were on holiday, we were sitting by the pool one day, drinking coke and listening to music and I wroted you a letter.' She made a mistake with the past tense of 'write'.

The normal development of language and communication skills shows a great deal of variation. Tom might use short phrases and ask questions while still being less than two years old, while Sam may not start using short phrases or asking questions until he is nearly four years old. The gap may seem enormous at age two and three, but by five years of age it has probably evened out, and it is possible that by then both may be at approximately the same level.

The development and expansion of children's language skills continues, going hand in hand with their growing experience.

# CHAPTER 3

# *Recognising Hearing Problems*

## Magdalene Moorey and Merle Mahon

This chapter is intended to clarify what is meant by a hearing loss, to describe the effect on developing speech and language, and consider ways in which such problems may be identified and managed.

## What is meant by 'hearing loss'?

Hearing ability is usually measured in terms of the quietest sound levels that can be detected for different frequencies (**pitches** or **tones**). The doctor or audiologist compares the hearing of an individual to a 'normal' value: 'normal' hearing is described as the quietest sounds which can be heard by young healthy adults. When sounds have to be made louder than normal before a person can detect those sounds, then it is customary to describe that person as having a hearing loss. This can range in severity from **mild** to **profound** or **total**. The term **deaf** usually implies a hearing loss sufficient to interfere with normal conversation and which may be helped by a hearing aid of some sort. Approximately one in a thousand children are born with this sort of loss.

Possible causes of a hearing loss may be: an inherited disorder; damage resulting from an infection during pregnancy, such as Rubella; or from drugs which are given to treat a severe, possibly life-threatening illness such as meningitis, but which prove to be damaging to the hearing mechanism; or diseases of the middle ear. Some hearing loss remains unexplained.

## The hearing mechanism

The hearing mechanism can be thought of as having two parts; a **conductive** part (the outer and middle ear) and a **sensory** part (the inner ear).

The conductive part includes the ear drum and the chain of tiny bones in the middle ear. Its function is broadly to conduct sound energy from outside to the inner ear.

The sensory part includes the coiled sense organ known as the **cochlea** in which are arranged the cells which convey sound as electrical energy up to the brain.

It helps to think of the conductive part as a 'mechanical' system of levers, drums and moving parts, and the sensory part as a 'nervous' system of wires connections and 'electrical current'.

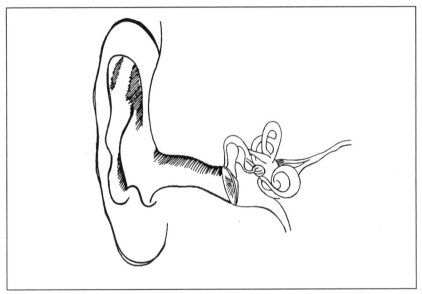

**Figure 3.1** Outer, middle and inner ear

## Damage to the hearing mechanism

The severity of the hearing loss, the loss over different frequencies and the possibilities for restoring hearing, all depend on where the system has been damaged.

Damage to the outer or middle ear results in **Conductive Hearing Loss**. This can be mild to moderate in severity. Generally all frequencies are affected and the outcome for hearing is that sound is 'muffled'. Complex sound such as speech would be difficult to understand, with the quieter consonants for example, 'f, sh, p' almost disappearing. Making the sound louder usually helps and there are often surgical and medical procedures which can be employed to improve the system. The conditions which give rise to conductive loss are frequently temporary and as such the hearing levels may improve with or without intervention.

Damage to the inner ear results in **Sensori-neural Hearing Loss**. This can range from mild to profound or total loss. Hearing for different frequencies (or tones) tends to be affected to varying degrees; generally, high frequencies are more severely affected. This means that as well as sound being perceived as quieter there is also distortion in what is heard. Consequently, making sound louder, particularly complex sound such as speech, does not necessarily make it any easier to understand. As sensori-neural hearing loss involves damage to the nervous system as opposed to the mechanical system there is frequently little that can be done to 'restore' that function. A hearing aid may be helpful in making use of the hearing function that still remains, but the loss is permanent.

Sensori-neural hearing loss is rare in the U.K., approximately 1:1000, according to an EEC Study conducted by Davis in 1993, and a nursery nurse or teacher may meet in their career only a small number of children with this sort of loss. Conductive hearing loss is by contrast extremely common in young children (Haggard and Hughes 1991).

## Middle ear dysfunction

Middle ear dysfunction is a term which can be used to describe any difficulty in the normal working of the middle ear. Research has shown that the majority of children have at least one episode of middle ear dysfunction which can result in hearing loss before their third birthday (Haggard, Birkin and Pringle 1993) and that some children go on to have repeated episodes of middle ear dysfunction.

There are two usual causes of these episodes of middle ear dysfunction.

1. The passage which connects the middle ear to the nose (the **Eustachian Tube**) may become blocked. The fresh supply of air necessary to keep the middle ear healthy is thus removed, and within a matter of weeks the middle ear can become fluid-filled and unable to adequately perform its function of conveying sound to the cochlea. If

this state fails to correct itself, or if no treatment is offered, a condition called **Otitis Media with Effusion**, or **Glue Ear** may develop.

2. The middle ear may become painfully infected. This is called **Supperative Otitis Media**. Failure to treat this condition may result in a burst ear drum and other severe medical complications.

These middle ear conditions, known collectively as 'Otitis Media' are much more common in young children. This is because young children have immature mechanisms for fighting infections; and because the efficiency of mechanical functioning of the Eustachian tube can easily be reduced for a number of reasons, such as the horizontal angle of the Eustachian tubes in infants and young children (Gibbin, 1993) – see Figure 3.2. Such problems are also more common in the winter months, and occur more frequently in children who have had low birth weight. Certain groups of children are particularly prone to middle ear dysfunction for example, children with a cleft palate or Down's Syndrome.

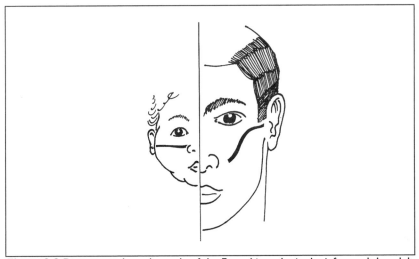

**Figure 3.2** Diagram to show the angle of the Eustachian tube in the infant and the adult

### *Treatment of middle ear dysfunction*

Many doctors employ a policy of 'wait and see' with middle ear problems in childhood. They are usually working on the basis that most children grow out of these problems in time, and that there is little conclusive evidence that treating the condition actively, by medical or surgical means, has any effect on whether children will go on to have further episodes of middle ear dysfunction. Having said this, it is worth reviewing briefly the most common treatments.

### Treatment with drugs

Antibiotics may be prescribed, either to clear an infection inside the middle ear space, or to reduce swelling in the tonsils or adenoids which may be the cause of the Eustachian tube being blocked. If antibiotics are prescribed, it is very important that they are given for long enough, and that the course is completed, to give maximum chance of all infection being cleared up; otherwise the infection may well reappear within a very short space of time.

Antihistamines or decongestants may be used if the blockage is thought to be caused by an allergic reaction in the cells which line the nose, throat and ear. These may be given in the form of nose drops which are extremely difficult to administer properly to a young child. A parent or nursery nurse asked to give nose drops to a child should ask for a demonstration of how this should be done to ensure that the drops actually reach the parts of the nose where the problem lies.

### Treatment with surgery

If the middle ear problems are being caused by swollen tonsils or adenoids an Ear, Nose and Throat (E.N.T.) surgeon may recommend their removal. This has the double effect of getting rid of a site of repeated infection and removing the mechanical obstruction to the Eustachian tube.

The surgeon may also decide to insert a ventilation tube or **grommet** into the ear drum. The grommet is placed so that it sits in the ear drum like a tiny window. This is not, as many mistakenly believe, to allow fluid to drain out of the middle ear through the ear drum, but rather to ensure a fresh supply of air to the middle ear. It is in effect acting as an alternative Eustachian tube. Thus, if the true eustachian tube should fail, for whatever reason, the middle ear remains healthy and air-filled. The grommets will eventually fall out, of their own accord, but this may take from six weeks to two years to happen. On average they remain in place for at least six months.

## What to look for in a child with hearing problems

The following points might alert an observant carer or teacher to the possibility of a hearing problem.

1. The child does not turn when called.
2. Hearing seems to change from day to day – sometimes s/he will turn to speech at normal conversational levels, other times only to a yell.
3. The child seems particularly attentive to visual cues, for example, watching the speaker's face.
4. The child's behaviour changes noticeably – a normally friendly, settled child becomes aggressive or tearful and withdrawn.
5. The child is distracted easily without one-to-one attention. In a group s/he may wander off, or be a step behind the other children, watching to see what to do next.
6. The child shows a marked difference in responsiveness in quiet conditions compared to where there is a lot of background noise.
7. Language development may be slowed down, or seem to deteriorate after a cold. Speech might be hard to understand, and the sentence structures the child uses might be simpler than those of his/her peers
8. The child may complain of painful ears, or pull at his/her ears or complain of them 'popping'.
9. The television may need to be turned up, or the child may sit very near to it to hear.
10. The child's voice volume may alter.

## Middle ear problems and language development

As stated above, the effect of a permanent, significant hearing loss which starts around birth has major implications for spoken language learning. The child may have difficulty in both understanding what is said, and in being understood. Language development may follow broadly the expected developmental route, but at a much slower pace, and there may be difficulties with using the speech sounds of the language at an age when a child might have been expected to have mastered these skills.

The case for language learning difficulties in the presence of middle ear problems is much less clear cut, despite a great deal of research dedicated to this issue. Much of this research is reviewed by Haggard, Birkin and Pringle (1993). The questions that have been asked are:

- 'Does middle ear dysfunction (with subsequent minor, fluctuating hearing loss) cause difficulty with language learning?';

- 'If it does cause difficulty, what particular aspects of communication are affected?';
- 'If there is an effect, is it a permanent one?'

This is not the place to recount the many difficulties involved in attempting to answer these questions, but it is fair to say that many of the conclusions drawn are dubious, and should be seriously questioned, because of errors or oversights in the way the studies were carried out. Looking at the literature as a whole it is possible to draw the following conservative conclusions:

- Middle ear dysfunction and consequent hearing loss may have a negative effect on language learning. This is particularly so when there are other factors present which predispose the child to language learning difficulties; factors such as, similar difficulties in the immediate family, or evidence of some neurological trauma (Bishop and Edmundson 1986).
- Where a language learning effect has been noticed, it seems to be greatest where the child had a history of middle ear dysfunction beginning before the first birthday.
- Most studies indicate a delay in developing spoken language skills.
- Those few studies which have followed children through to the primary school years suggest that these children have 'outgrown' their spoken language difficulties.
- There is some suggestion that these children may have more difficulty than their peers in learning to read. (For more detail see Webster, 1986).

Having said all this, it is possible for a child to have middle ear dysfunction with very little noticeable effect on hearing. Similarly, a child may have very slight middle ear dysfunction, a mild hearing loss and yet, be devastated by this, in terms of language learning and social development. There is not an easy one-to-one relationship between hearing loss and behavioural effects. In order to identify those children who are at risk of developing difficulties, identification procedures must look at both the hearing level and the behavioural effects; that is, it must look at listening behaviour and language skills.

## Identifying hearing problems

There are two main ways of identifying hearing problems in children:

1. The use of infant screening programmes aimed at picking out, at a moment in time, children who cannot perform a task as well as their 'normal' peers.

2. Picking out those children who, by their behaviour in an everyday setting, seem to be having difficulty with hearing, listening or communicating.

The first method will be carried out by health visitors or community medical officers. Its success relies on every child living in a specific area being tested in some way.

The second relies on informed individuals such as parents, nursery nurses, teachers, child minders, who know a particular child and who have expectations of what children ought to be 'doing' at a particular stage of their development.

### Formal assessment of hearing

In the U.K., most health authorities carry out a screening test of hearing on children aged approximately 7–8 months. This is known as the **Distraction Test of Hearing** and is usually carried out at a health centre or community clinic, by health visitors (McCormick, 1993). The baby is seated on the mother's knee and sounds are presented behind, and to the left and right sides of the baby's head. The baby must turn in response to each sound presented to pass the test. If s/he fails to turn, the test may be repeated one or two weeks later. If the baby still fails to turn to any sounds, then s/he will be referred to an Audiology clinic for full diagnostic assessment.

Many authorities carry out another screening test at three years which checks both hearing and language development. Here the child has to perform tasks, for example, to put a man in a boat, or a brick in a basket, in response to an auditory signal such as, 'go' or 's' which are presented at very quiet or 'minimal' sound levels.

A second test of hearing for speech may be carried out where the child has to point to a toy that is named very quietly. If the child does not respond at these very quiet levels then again the child is referred for diagnostic testing.

The child's health records should include the results of these assessments which will give some indication of hearing status over time. The fact that a child has passed these tests does not conclusively mean that there are no hearing difficulties. It may be that the child was tested on a 'good day' and that two weeks later hearing levels were beginning to fall. It may be that the child has acquired some hearing problem, either through a fall or as a result of some medication, or it may be that the initial tests were inaccurate. McCormick (1993) has shown how easy it is for a deaf baby to pass the Distraction Test because of inaccuracies in the way the test is carried out. For more detail, see McCormick, 1993; or Tucker and Nolan, 1984.

## The nursery school and hearing problems

The local authority day nursery system in the U.K. provides a limited number of places for pre-school children. Priority in placement is given to children who are more likely to be at a social disadvantage compared to their peers, or have some special need which the authorities feel can be met through day nursery place provision. Coupled with this, there are several reasons why the pre-school population as a whole may be high risk for hearing problems.

- This age group of children is also the age when children are most likely to have middle ear dysfunction.
- Children in a nursery or school may be more likely to pick up and pass on recurrent infections which make them more prone to middle ear problems. It is not possible to make any environment infection-free, but the risk is increased when children who are more likely to succumb to infection are spending long periods of the day together.
- If the child's parent(s) need to go out to work it may be more difficult to keep all the child's health appointments. It may seem more important to a parent to take time off for the child to be immunised than for the child to have a hearing check, when there has been no clear indication that there is anything wrong with the child's hearing. Parents who say, 'I know he's not deaf, he just listens when he wants to,' may miss 'minor' losses of hearing that fluctuate.

The nursery and school setting pose particular difficulties for a child with hearing problems:

1. Noise levels where young children gather can be excruciating. Many nursery nurses and teachers say they get used to this and do not notice it. This may lead to background noise being higher than it needs to be, for example, a radio may be left on, or it may mean that mild fluctuations in the child's hearing levels go unnoticed.

2. However dedicated and vigilant, it is not possible for a teacher to be as

responsive to day-to-day changes in any individual child's hearing in a classroom as it is for a parent at home.

3. There are many factors which affect a child's behaviour (see Chapter 6) and it may be that aggression or tearfulness is wrongly attributed to difficulties in adjusting to being one of a group of children, rather than the difficulty involved in coping with changing hearing levels.

## Ways of helping the child with a hearing loss

Having listed some of the difficulties a child might have in coping with a hearing loss in a group setting, it is also possible to draw up a list of ways to overcome these difficulties. The nursery or school can also provide positive ways of helping the child with hearing loss, whether fluctuating or permanent.

- If you suspect a child of having a hearing loss, ask the parent whether the child has had, and passed, the routine tests of hearing at 8 months, three years and five years.
- If the child has failed these, or is not at the appropriate age for a test, ask the parent if they could take the child to the doctor for referral to the hearing assessment clinic (Audiology clinic); this usually takes place in a child health clinic or health centre.
- Mention your suspicions about the hearing loss to the Community Medical Officer or school doctor when they visit the nursery/school.
- Follow up any requests with inquiries as to the outcome an any treatment.
- Reduce background noise to the minimum possible; turn off the radio if no-one is listening to it, arrange the room so that story time can take place in a quiet corner away from traffic noise, and have any child you suspect might be having difficulty at the front of the group near to the story-teller.
- Try and arrange the day's timetable so that each child has a chance to play or work in a small group, following adult direction, rather than always in big groups.
- Maintain good lighting in the room and try to face the child when you are giving instructions.
- Gain the child's attention before beginning to speak, either by calling their name or by saying: 'Are you ready? Are you listening?'
- Include some activities in the day's routine that involve the child responding to speech sounds and sounds which are not speech sounds such as, marching to a drum, matching the sounds of musical

instruments, 'Ready, Steady, Go!' games.

- Try some of these games at quiet levels so that the child learns to use his/her hearing during 'good' phases. Ask the visiting speech and language therapist for some activities and ideas for group games.

- All staff should be aware of the child's difficulties, and any suspicions regarding his/her hearing, so that they all deal with the child in a consistent way.

- If the child has been prescribed some medication make sure that you continue with this and if necessary ask the medical officer to show you how to best administer nose drops.

# CHAPTER 4

## How to Recognise Speech and Language Problems

### Rosemarie MorganBarry and Jannet A. Wright

Chapter 2 outlined the normal pattern of speech and language development and described the many varied aspects of human communication. When the complexity of the speech and language system is considered, it is amazing that the majority of children manage to enter school at 5 years of age with communication skills that enable them to cope with school life. Some of these children may have been slow to acquire language initially, but 'caught up' in the pre-school years. There are, however, other children whose poor speech and language skills are a cause of anxiety to their parents and to the professionals who care for them, both before and after school entry.

This chapter is concerned with the early recognition of children whose language is slow to develop. Behaviour patterns may be an indication that a child is having problems learning language. It is these behaviours which will be described. This should help professionals caring for such children to be aware of possible speech-language problems and to ask for specialist help for the child as early as possible.

There are two important questions to be considered concerning speech and language in children.

First, how well do children understand the language heard around them? Second, how well can children use speech and language so that other people know what they are saying?

When reading about speech and language delay, 'understanding' is frequently referred to as **reception** or **comprehension** of language, and 'being understood' as the **expression** of language (see Chapter 2). Each aspect will be considered in turn, with guidelines and a checklist to highlight possible problems in learning language.

# Understanding

Some children have difficulty understanding what is said to them. This may be because they have problems with hearing (see Chapter 3), or because they are learning English as a second language, having previously used a different language at home (for example, Bengali, Cantonese, Turkish, Tigrina). However, even without hearing difficulties, or learning English as a second language, some children are slow in learning to talk, and their understanding is not as good as might be expected for their age.

Children who have problems in understanding are often helped by the 'clues' given to them by adult speakers. These clues may include pointing, gesture, facial expression. In addition, the situation within the home/nursery or school may provide clues for such a child. For example, the instruction: 'Put your coat on, Tommy,' may be accompanied by pointing to the coat-rack, or even holding out the coat. Similarly, questions may be asked, or instructions given, relating to various activities, when the objects being talked about are in front of, or near to the child. For example:

- 'Find the red engine Matthew.'
- 'Mary, where's the scissors?'
- 'Are you going to put some yellow paint on your picture?'
 'What are you doing to teddy, Simon?'

The same may happen with general instructions, such as those given below, which are all part of the routine of the day, and which most children quickly learn, without needing to understand the individual words. For example:

- 'It's tidy – up time.'
- 'Wash your hands for dinner.'
- 'Come and sit down for story-time.'

Adults, when talking to children, are for the most part unaware of how much help is provided by these 'clues'; they occur naturally and without our thinking about them too much. Try giving someone directions about a route they have to follow, without using your hands.

These clues, gestures and facial expressions can be useful; think about how much you can guess about what's going on when you visit a country where you don't know a word of the language. Children with poor understanding are in just that situation, they rely on these additional clues to help them make sense of what is going on around them.

However, the use of these clues make it difficult for us to know exactly how much speech and language a child understands. Recently, two teachers made these observations about the same boy:

'He understands everything that's going on.'
'He doesn't understand a word I say.'

These comments seem to be in total disagreement, but, in fact, both may be true. The boy probably could understand everything that was going on, by watching for the 'clues'; or, it may be that the situation was very familiar to him; but he may not have understood much of what the second teacher actually said. Thus, if asked a question such as, 'Have you got a pet at home, Sean?', unexpectedly, 'out of the blue', it might well have met with nothing more than a blank stare from Sean.

Children with poor understanding can work extremely hard to try and follow instructions. One way they may help themselves may be to watch other children and copy them. In the classroom this may mean that they are last to start an activity or follow an instruction. They may attend to, or hear, only the last word, or words, in a sentence and appear to ignore part of what was said.

In order to establish how much spoken language a child is actually understanding, it is necessary to try and cut out all these additional, helpful clues, and to assess the child's ability to comprehend, using words alone.

When children are learning to talk it is quite common for them to repeat what they have just heard, this is part of learning, and is to be encouraged. However, a child who frequently 'echoes' what was said, and who constantly repeats what adults or children are saying, may have a serious comprehension problem as illustrated below:

Teacher: 'Is it your birthday today?'
Child :  'Birthday.'
Teacher: 'Yes, you're four today!'
Child :  'Four today.'
Teacher: 'Did you have many presents?'
Child :  'Many presents.'

### What to look for

- The child who is slow to learn the class routine.
- The child who watches and copies others.
- The child with poor attention at story-time.

- The child who 'echoes'.
- The child who often makes an inappropriate response to questions and instructions.

These behaviours could also indicate learning difficulties and /or lack of confidence, and need to be investigated in more detail.

### *How to check:*

- Give simple instructions, without clues, and note the child's response.
- Ask the occasional question, 'out of the blue'.
- Give more complex directions, and possibly unexpected instructions and note exactly what the child does: for example: 'Go to the cupboard and get a piece of blue paper;'or 'Put your toys away before you go outside;' or 'Put a lego brick on the desk before you go outside.'

### *What to do:*

- Ask for the child's hearing to be checked (See Chapter 3).
- Ask about language(s) spoken at home.
- Refer to a speech and language therapist.
- Check child has understood an instruction by asking them to repeat what you have just said.
- Watch closely to see if the child's response is appropriate for your instructions.
- Use short simple instructions.
- Make use of every day gesture to aid understanding.

### Being understood

There are a number of important aspects of speech and language, all of which are necessary in order to be understood when talking to other people. These are :

    – the sounds (**articulation**), which make up
    – the words (**vocabulary**) which must be in
    – the right order (**syntax**) and,
    – appropriate to the situation (**pragmatics**).

(The words in brackets are explained more fully in Chapter 2).
If any of these areas are not working properly, or are poorly developed,

then communication can break down. The speaker will not be able to get the message across and this can become a serious problem as the child gets older.

Each of these areas will be considered in turn.


## Articulation

This area is concerned with a child's mastery of the sounds of the language (see Chapter 2). Young children take time, literally, to get their tongues round the sounds of the language, and many – but not all – children practise these sounds in the babbling stage of infancy as described in Chapter 2. Some sounds are easier to make than others:

/m/ as in mummy, more
/n/ as in nana, no
/b/ as in baby, bye
/d/ as in daddy

These are all quite straightforward and are usually the first sounds a child produces.

Slightly more difficult sounds are:

/k/ (written also as 'c') as in kitten, car
/g/ as in go

while the following sounds are all quite difficult:

/f/ as in finger
/v/ as in van
/s/ as in sun, sea
/ch/as in chip
/r/ as in rabbit
/sh/ as in shoe, ship, sugar

Words and phrases in which a number of these more difficult sounds occur together require the tongue and lips to perform some quite difficult gymnastics; in a word like 'nana' there are only two sounds, which are repeated, and the tongue does not have a great deal to do, but in a phrase such as 'fish and chips,' there are nine different sounds:

'f- i- sh – a-n- ch-i-p-s' = 9 sounds

(when talking quickly you rarely say/hear the 'd' at the end of 'and'). All of this involves the tongue in some tricky manoeuvres. Try saying 'fish and chips' slowly to yourself and think about how you do it.

It is therefore not at all uncommon, or surprising, to hear young children producing immaturities such as:

'wabbit' for rabbit
'tip' for chip
'pi' or 'pit' for fish

Sometimes, they get some of the sounds right but put them in the wrong place. For example, Lisa aged three years could say:

'tis an fips' (fish and chips).

She managed the difficult /s/ and /f/ sounds, but got them in the wrong order. Other examples of getting sounds the wrong way round in a word are:

'efalant' elephant
'tefalone' telephone
'hostipul' hospital.

Other common immaturities include:

'tar' car
'dot' got
and words in which the tongue comes forward in a lisp as in:
'thun' sun
'thock' sock

Sometimes children miss the /s/ at the beginning of some words, for example:

'poon' spoon
'tar' star
'carf' scarf.

This is because the second sound of the word is a **consonant** and the tongue and lips have some difficult manoeuvres to make. It is easier to say words in which a **vowel** follows a consonant, as in:

'c a r' 's a y' 't oo l' 'n ai l'

than to say words where two consonants occur next to each other, as in:

'sc a r' 'st a y' 'st oo l' 'sn ai l'

especially when one of the two consonants in the consonant cluster is the difficult /s/ sound.

By the time children near their fourth birthday, many of the immature pronunciations should have disappeared.

For further reading about this see Crystal, 1986, Chapter 3.

## Phonology

This is related to articulation and the speech sounds of the language. The word 'phonology' is used by speech and language therapists to refer to the way in which individual sounds are put together to make words, such that changing a sound within a word will make a change in meaning. For example: children learn quite early on (see Chapter 2) that there is a difference between

'*p*ear' and '*b*ear'
'*c*at' and '*h*at'
'mou*th*' and 'mou*se*'
'p*u*ppy' and 'p*o*ppy'
'Da*nn*y' and 'Da*dd*y'
'do*g*' and 'do*gs*'

By changing (or adding) one sound in each of these pairs of words (known as **minimal pairs**) there is a resultant change of meaning.

Most children learn how the sound system of the language works, but how they do this is one of the wonders of child language development. Nobody teaches them how to recognise that different sounds make different meanings; they learn the rules of phonology in much the same way as they work out for themselves the rules of grammar (see chapter 2). The context in which the words are used help to make the meaning clear, although this may not always work.

The examples of the pronunciations given earlier showed that, although young children may be aware of how sounds in a language work together to make words and change meaning, they do not in the very early years have the necessary ability to put their lips and tongues around the sounds to give the complete adult pronunciation.

Other children may have different problems. Children with hearing problems (see chapter 3) have difficulty hearing the small differences that carry meaning; they may therefore be unable to produce them accurately, thus making their speech hard to understand. Some children whose hearing for everyday sounds seems adequate may have particular difficulty in distinguishing the small differences between sounds: /p/ and /b/; /f/ and /v/. Also sounds like 'tr' as in '*tr*ain' and 'ch' as in '*ch*ain' may sound very alike unless you listen closely. Speech and language therapists, therefore, use tests containing sets of minimal pairs of words (MorganBarry, 1988) to check how well children hear and discriminate the differences between them.

Some children, although able to discriminate speech sounds, nonetheless use only a few sounds to do the work of many.

Gary aged three years nine months used the /g/ sound most of the time. For example he would say:

'I wan go geep bu egun maging goig.'
[I want(to) go (to) sleep but everyone (is) making (a) noise.]

He uses the [g] sound instead of /sl/ in 'sleep', /v/ in 'everyone', /k/ in 'making', /n/ at the beginning and /z/ at the end of 'noise'. (He also missed some words out – see **syntax** below.)

All this makes his speech very hard to understand. His mother could understand him, but other family members and friends often had to ask for a translation. This is because his mother has got used to Gary's style of pronunciation. People who are in daily contact with such children may become familiar with their unusual speech; this does not necessarily mean that the children are speaking more clearly, but that the listener has become more used to their speech patterns.

These speech patterns are called 'phonological systems'; a child may have his own phonological system which changes and develops as he gradually acquires more sounds, and as he learns to fit these sounds together to match the adult phonological system of the language. Not all children manage this task; they are then described as having a 'phonological disorder'.

Phonological disorders may occur in different ways. For example, there are children who may not have all of the sounds, like Stacey aged four who said:

'Dit my pable, I'm puttin tup om it.'
[This (is) my table, I'm putting cup(s) on it.]

Other children, however, may have most, or all, of the sounds, but use them so variably that they remain unintelligible. If, in addition, they omit certain sounds, the result is a problem for the listener. This sentence from Michelle, age seven, is an example:

'You dot one bat tipey tot an one bap potty pok'

meaning:

'You've got one black stripey sock and one black spotty sock'.

It is important to remember that while many children grow out of early speech difficulties, some need help before they get to school, where teachers and other children expect them to be able to communicate clearly. Simple problems like lisping may sort themselves out, but parents, teachers and nursery staff need to be alert to children, like Gary and Stacey, who have more complex problems. Some children who have speech difficulties which are complex, severe or unusual may later experience difficulty with reading, writing and spelling. For further reading on this topic, see Snowling (1987).

### What to llok for

- The child who cannot be understood by adults outside the family.
- The child who sounds 'muddled.'
- The child who appears to have only a few sounds.
- The child who says the same word differently at different times.

### How to check

- Look at a book or pictures with a child in a quiet corner and listen to him/her. It is important to listen carefully because it is easy to think the child has said a word correctly when you have understood what s/he has said.
- Name pictures for the child and encourage him/her to imitate you – notice how each word is said.

### What to do

- Ask for the child's hearing to be checked.
- Ask whether family and friends have commented on the child's speech.
- Refer to the speech and language therapist.
- Do not mimic the child to their face.
- Do not repeat the incorrect pronunciation to the child but say the word correctly in a sentence following their incorrect attempt.

### Vocabulary

Some children do not have the words or vocabulary which one might expect for their age. For example, John aged six years was looking at a book with his mother.

Mother: Oh look, there's a...
John:  That.
Mother: Yes, it's a car.
John:  Car.
Mother: They're going on the...
John :  That.
Mother: Yes, the road.

When talking about the pictures John appears not to have the vocabulary to describe the picture. By the age of four years one would expect a child to name objects that they can see in a picture, and talk about some of the actions. John's responses are more typical of the majority of children aged two and a half, rather than a year year old.

Children's first words are awaited with eager anticipation by the adults around them, they are often recorded in a book. When children are first learning to talk their parents can easily remember the words they can say. But, very quickly it becomes impossible to keep track as children's vocabulary grows at such a rapid rate (Crystal, 1986).

An activity, such as the one John is doing, naming pictures in a book, is often more appropriate with children in the first two to three years of life. It provides them with the opportunity to learn and practise new words. This is why they frequently choose the same book for adults to read to them, so that they have a chance to practise or rehearse new vocabulary. By the time they are John's age they are more interested in listening to and retelling a story.

Children who appear to have difficulty learning new words, or remembering words, could have a language delay. Their speech may sound clear and their sentence structures appear appropriate for what they want to say, but their vocabulary may not be increasing in the way one would expect.

### What to look for

- A child who finds it hard to remember the names of objects and the names of other children in the class.
- A child who has trouble learning new words.
- A child who uses 'this'/'that' a great deal without naming items/objects.
- A child who is not always fluent (see chapter 5).

*How to check*

- Choose an unfamiliar book or toy to look at with the child. After talking about a few of the pictures or items see if the child can tell you what they are. Try again the next day, and again the day after.
- If a child cannot name an object see if he/she can tell you what it is used for.

*What to do*

- Choose a topic such as fruit, transport or animals and draw the child's attention to certain words during a week. See if they remember them in two weeks time.
- Find out if remembering or learning new words is a problem in other situations, for example, playschool, nursery, school or with grandparents.
- Ask the speech and language therapist to see the child.
- See Chapters 8 and 9.

*Syntax*

Paul aged four years explained how his father was carrying out some do-it-yourself.

'My dad out went hammer, got hammer wood got down.'

Paul manages to get his message across, but the words are not in the order we would expect. It sounds strange. In English words are put in a certain order in a sentence, this is the grammar or syntax of the language. If children have difficulties in this area their sentences may be very short in length or they may sound 'odd' because the order is incorrect. Sometimes children talk using the correct sounds, and, as the adult can understand what they are saying, it is easy to ignore the fact that the words are not in the right order. The following sentence shows this:

Mary aged five years: 'Mummy, ice cream me have?'
Mother:                'Later, when we go to the shops.'

Mary's mother understands that Mary is asking for an ice cream, she is used to Mary's syntax, but to a stranger this would sound unusual.

It is more common for children to have both poor articulation and syntax, which makes it very difficult for the listener to understand their speech. Remember the examples of Gary and Stacey given earlier in this chapter.

### Telegrammatic speech

Sometimes when listening to a very young child or an older child who has difficulty with syntax the listener is aware that the child's speech sounds rather like a verbal telegram. This type of speech in fact has been called **telegrammatic speech**, and you can see why if you read the examples below:

'Me go school now,' instead of: 'I go to school now;'
'Daddy go work car,' instead of: 'Daddy goes to work in the car.'

In these examples the children retain the words which carry the information in the sentence. It does sound like a telegram, where to save expense one omits the unnecessary words.

However, if children have a problem with syntax, they are unlikely to leave out words from choice, it is more likely that cannot cope with a longer utterance, or that they have failed to learn the linking words.

The linking words in the phrases above include 'to, in, the'. If a child is two years old the omission of these linking words would not cause concern. At this age children string together the important words so that when telling an adult what they intend to do, 'Me go garden,' is perfectly acceptable. However, if a child was still doing this at four years old, then there would be cause for concern because at this age you would expect to hear, 'I want to go in the garden.'

The following example indicates a severe problem in a five year old boy, describing an outing with his parents:

'Mummy, daddy, me went car, long time, shops, ice-cream new shirt.'

This child gets his message across, but the listener has to do a lot of work in order to understand that he meant:

– Mummy, daddy and child went in the car;
– it was a long way to town;
– the child had an ice-cream in a restaurant;
– a new shirt was bought for the child.

If you suspect a child is having problems with syntax, the following suggestions may help.

### What to look for

- A child missing words out of a sentence.
- A child who gets words in the wrong order in a sentence.
- A child whose speech sounds a bit like a telegram.

*How to check*

- Listen carefully to children when they are telling a story, or talking about something they have just done.
- Note down exactly what they say, do not add in any extra words.
- Look at your notes; have they left any words out? or are any of the words in an order that surprises you?

*What to do*

- Provide the correct, full length version of the child's sentence after they have spoken to you, but do not expect them to repeat it. (See 'Modelling' Chapter 2).
- Ask the speech and language therapist to see the child.
- Do not mimic the child's speech.

Children who have problems, or who are delayed in learning to talk, often have all these types of difficulty together: difficulties with sounds, with vocabulary, with syntax. These are the children who are, 'reluctant communicators', who say little, often only speaking one or two words at a time; who point and use gesture to help them 'ask' for what they want, and who are unwilling to talk with people they do not know well.

*Pragmatics*

Conversation is not just two people talking, each saying something in turn; what they say should be linked in some way. If it is not linked, it is like a crossed line on the telephone with two unconnected conversations going on.

A normal conversation with a four year old would go something like this:

| Sam aged four years: | 'I got new shoes.' |
| Teacher: | 'Did you? How nice.' |
| Sam: | 'Yes, they're red. |
| Teacher: | 'Where did you get them?' |
| Sam: | 'My mum and me went to the shop.' |

Now look at this conversation between Tracy aged five years and her teacher:

Tracy:  'I got new shoes.'

Teacher: 'Did you? How nice.'
Tracy:   'I got new shoes.'
Teacher: 'I know, you just told me.'
Tracy:   'I'm doing painting now.'

This conversation is not as successful as the one with Sam and it is typical of Tracy's conversations with both adults and children. Tracy knows how to attract adult attention, but cannot maintain the conversation. A successful continuation of this exchange would probably have involved Tracy pointing to the shoes and getting the adult to look at them, instead of repeating her first statement.

Pragmatics refers to the **use of language**, how we choose an appropriate way of talking, depending on the situation we find ourselves in. You might ask a child to shut the door by saying:

'Shut the door please, Timmy.'

To an adult you might say any of these:

'Could you shut the door?'
'Would you mind shutting the door?'
'Do you want to shut the door?'

You probably use a different style of speech to adults you know well, such as family members and friends, than to those you are meeting for the first time. Children usually learn these differences quite unconsciously, but some children have to be taught appropriate use of language.

When talking to children who have difficulty in the pragmatic area of language, a number of features may be apparent. They may have particular difficulty in linking their responses to the other speakers comments. For example, when doing some craft work at school, the teacher said, 'Look, the paper has stuck to the table.' The response from the child was, 'We've got yellow tables like this at home.'

They are poor at taking turns in a conversation – so they constantly interrupt and their comments are not related. It is normal for young children to interrupt if they see or hear something novel such as a fire engine or airship going by, but, by school entry, constant interruptions and inappropriate comments may signal a problem. Such children may also have difficulty taking turns in games in the classroom or any group activities.

They may not know how to attract the adult's attention when starting a conversation. Children without any problems may call out to the adult passing by, or say, 'Guess what!' 'Look,' or 'See this,' or they may pull an adult's sleeve. A child who finds it difficult, or is unable to attract adult attention, may start talking without looking at the adult. It may sound as if they are talking to themselves. The adult eventually becomes aware that the child is talking to them and that a response is needed.

They may not know how to talk about a person or object which is not present. Such children assume that the listener knows what they are referring to. To the listener it may feel like they are coming into a conversation half way through.

They can have difficulty linking topics in a conversation and if the conversation breaks down they do not know how to start it up again or 'repair' it.

### *What to look for*

- A child who has problems taking turns in a conversation.
- A child whose conversation continually moves from one topic to the next, fairly rapidly, for no reason.
- A child who cannot switch topics and goes on and on about a subject.
- A classroom environment which may be adding to the child's problems. The adult's language may be too complex, there may not be enough time for the child to understand what is said to them and for them to respond.

### *How to check*

- Listen to the child in conversation with another adult.
- Listen to the child in conversation with another child, and with a group of children.
- Watch how the child gets adult attention.
- Note if the child is able to take turns in the conversation.
- Look at the complexity of the adult's language. This may be causing a breakdown in communication, because the child is not understanding what the adult is saying.

### *What to do*

- This is a very complex area of communication to help. It is therefore best to ask a speech and language therapist to see the child.

## Summary

This chapter outlines some of the reasons why it can be hard to identify a child who has difficulty understanding speech and language.

Examples are given of problems which can occur with articulation, vocabulary, syntax and pragmatics.

It is important to remember that, as listeners, we are good at interpreting what we hear people say to us. When talking with children, the most important aspect is listening to what they say, so we can respond appropriately. But, in order to watch out for potential difficulties, we also have to learn to listen to how they say it.

Adults who work with children are in the frontline of identifying speech and language problems. It is often the child's behaviour, such as temper tantrums and/or withdrawal from speech situations, that cause adults to suspect a delay in development.

If you have any concerns at all about a child's speech and language, then refer them to the local speech and language therapist.

# CHAPTER 5

# Stammering in Young Children

## Renée Byrne

'Don't worry, he'll grow out of it.' This advice may be given to parents of children who are starting to stammer. Some children do grow out of it, but some do not. Equally, some parents stop worrying, and some do not. Parents may feel anxiety about their child's speech which is out of all proportion to the problem, because they feel helpless and guilty and do not know what to do.

This chapter explains what is happening when children stammer, and advice is offered about what may be done to help the child at home, in the nursery or at school. Questions that speech and language therapists are frequently asked will be answered, and suggestions will be made about what to do and what not to do when a child's speech is not fluent.

## Stammering, stuttering and disfluency

There is no difference between stammering and stuttering. Which term you use is largely a matter of choice.

The term disfluent just means not fluent. All of us are disfluent at times, especially when tired, excited or confused about what we are trying to say; we all hesitate when speaking, insert 'mmm' and 'er', repeat sounds, and words. We get mixed up about what we want to say, or cannot choose sufficiently quickly between two words and so become stuck for a moment. This may be referred to as 'normal disfluency'. However, we are not stammering because, whereas *all stammering is disfluent, not all disfluency is stammering.*

If adults have episodes of disfluency in their speech, is it any wonder that the vast majority of children, before the age of five, go through a period of normal disfluency? Some children have little difficulty learning the complex skills required for the acquisition of speech and language (as discussed in Chapter 2); but for others, learning to speak is quite a struggle.

Just as children do not crawl across the floor at one moment and then immediately stand up and walk down the stairs without constantly falling, picking themselves up and trying again, so most children do not acquire speech and language without experiencing some difficulties. They stumble in their speech just as they stumble when learning to walk, they hesitate, repeat sounds, words and phrases, pause and try again. This is quite normal, and when it occurs in many children up to the age of 5, it is called **Normal Disfluency** (Van Riper, 1982). However, although the majority of children go through a period of normal disfluency, only 4 per cent-5 per cent show signs of the early stages of stammering (Andrews and Harris, 1964).

## What are the signs of early stammering?

*Repetitions:*
- of sounds, for example, m..m..m..mummy;
- of syllables, for example din..din..dinner;
- of words, for example more...more...more drink;
- of phrases, for example can I have, can I have?

Sound and syllable repetitions are more typically associated with stammering than are word, and phrase repetitions (Adams, 1977).

However, repetitions are heard in all children, and it is only when they are heard frequently that they may be considered to be a mild sign of stammering.

*Prolongations* or holding on to sounds such as 'r', 'l', 's', 'sh', 'f', as in: ffffffffffffather or lllllllittle.

The prolongation of sounds is less commonly heard in fluent speech than repetitions. When prolongations are heard in a child's speech they do not necessarily indicate that the child is stammering. They must be considered in the context of the whole of the child's speech pattern before they can be thought of as an early warning sign of stammering.

*Blocks* or 'getting stuck'. In this situation speech actually stops. This speech behaviour may cause distress to parents and, sometimes, momentary discomfort to the child. It is often an early sign of stammering. However, many other features of the child and his/her speech would be considered by a speech and language therapist before a diagnosis of 'stammering' is made.

*Struggle, tension and fear* – if children become aware of their speech difficulties, they may struggle and become tense in order to release themselves from the unpleasant sensations of the stammer. Struggle, tension and fear are a part of the beginning of true stammering, and help is required.

*Avoidance* – if children feel unhappy about their speech, then they may try to use tricks and devices to *avoid* and *hide* the stammer from other people. They may avoid certain words by not using them or changing them for others, for example saying 'small' instead of 'little', or 'magic' instead of 'good'. They may avoid talking to certain people, particularly those in authority. Thus, when in class, they may not answer questions, or ask for things they need such as another piece of paper. Unfortunately, the more they try to avoid and hide, the more fearful they may become and so the stammer may tend to get worse. At the same time it may remain less noticeable to others, because it is largely hidden. Avoidance behaviour is a true sign of stammering because it is not a behaviour found in fluent people.

Repetitions, prolongations and blocks are heard in the speech of most young children, and it is only if they occur too frequently or with great severity that they may indicate the first, mild signs of stammering.

Struggle, tension, fear and avoidance tend to indicate that the child is stammering.

## What is the difference between normal disfluency and early stammering?

There are several tests and assessments which may be used by speech and language therapists in order to assess disfluent children, for example *Continuum of Disfluent Speech Behaviours* (Gregory and Hill, 1980); *Stuttering Prediction Instrument for Young Children* (Riley, 1981); *A Component Model for Treating Stuttering in Children* (Riley and Riley, 1984); and *A Chronicity Prediction Checklist* (Cooper, 1985). Most of these examine three important areas:

- The history of the child and the family. Questions will be asked about other members of the family who may stammer, about when the child began saying words, when the disfluency was first noticed, and whether the child's speech is getting better or worse.

- Attitudes, such as how the parents feel about their child's speech, and whether the child reacts to being disfluent.
- The speech of the child, including the frequency and duration of episodes of disfluency, as well as the child's language and articulatory skills.

The difference between normal disfluency and early stammering may not always be clear, but in this context it is important to note that the therapist would be concerned with the general speech and communicative skills of the child, and not just with the disfluent aspects.

### General speech

It is important to stress that research shows that many children who are thought to be stammering have difficulty in learning the words to express themselves (Murray and Reed, 1977) or they may be slow in mastering the fine, co-ordinating muscular movements needed to articulate the sounds of speech (Conture and Caruso, 1987). As adults, we are aware that when we cannot think of the right word to use, or when we do not know how to pronounce a word, we will hesitate and pause. It becomes obvious that a child who has a language delay or an articulatory difficulty is at risk of becoming disfluent.

Jim for example, is a very excited three and a half year old. He is at the zoo for the first time, where he sees an elephant. He desperately wants to tell his Mother about this huge, grey elephant, but he does not have the language to express the concept of 'huge', nor the articulatory competence to say a word like 'elephant'. So you may well hear that child saying, 'Mum...mum...mummy, look at the...the...the big...big mum...mmm the...the thing.'

Jim may be thought to be stammering, and may be sent to a speech and language therapist. However, as he is under five he may be normally disfluent, or he may have a language and/or articulation delay. The speech and language therapist will use specifically designed speech and language tests and assessments which may help in making such a decision.

If the speech and language therapist finds that Jim has begun to stammer then the question may be asked: Why does he stammer? There is no simple answer. There is rarely a single reason. A stammer is usually the result of a combination of different factors. The reasons why a child begins to stammer may be like a jigsaw puzzle – there are several pieces of varying sizes, but it is not until these pieces lock together that a stammer will occur.

Family history, attitudes and speech have been referred to above as areas which a speech and language therapist would need to assess, and these may help to form some of the pieces of the puzzle. Within these areas there are specific factors which may have special significance in making the pieces lock together:

- *High Self-Expectations* – Some children try to be perfect, and tend to blame themselves for all sorts of everyday problems that arise at home or at school.
- *Articulatory Problems* – Some children have difficulties in co-ordinating the speech mechanism to produce rapid and accurate sounds and syllables.
- *Disruptive Communication Environment* – Children's speech may be disturbed by the attitudes and behaviour of people in their environment, especially if these are people with whom they need to communicate.
- *Unrealistic Parental Expectations* – The standards of general behaviour, and of speech, which the parents expect may be too high for the child to attain.

## When should a disfluent child be referred to a speech and language therapist?

Children as young as two to two and a half years old are now regularly referred to the speech and language therapist. If this seems young to you, then it is important to understand the therapist's role with children within this age group. In general, children should be referred to a speech and language therapist as soon as the parent, carer, nursery nurse, teacher or other significant adult becomes concerned about their speech over a period of time. If the adult is specifically concerned about the child's disfluency, then, recent research shows that the earlier the child is referred, the greater are the chances of permanent fluency (Myers & Woodford (1992); Riley & Riley (1984).

With very young children, the therapist will discuss issues with parents or others involved, and will make an assessment through a play session where there is no raising of awareness and no pressure is placed on the child. If it is thought that there is a risk for long-term stammering, then a management programme will be suggested.

There are some general 'Do's' and 'Don't's' (see below), but the therapist will offer management strategies specific to that child and his/her environment, so that fluency may be enhanced and disfluency minimised by the speech behaviour that the child hears and not be any direct interference with his/her own speech. With older children, direct speech work may be undertaken in order to increase fluency. The therapist will always take great care not to create awareness or anxiety about disfluency where none exists.

### What is the difference between early stammering and stammering in the older child or adult?

Stammering is essentially a developmental problem and so grows and changes over time. Stammering has been compared to an iceberg (Sheehan 1970). Like an iceberg, stammering has a visible part, the speech symptoms, and the hidden part, the feelings and attitudes beneath the surface. It is essential when working with the child to consider the hidden part as well as the surface symptoms.

The amount showing above the surface at any one time can change, because the stammer and the feelings associated with it are not constant in any one person; they change according to circumstances.

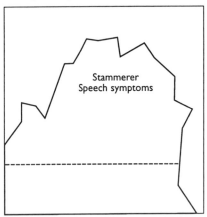

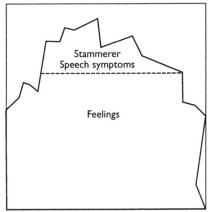

**Figure 5.1** Iceberg A The young child

**Figure 5.2** Iceberg B The older child or adult

Figure 5.1 illustrates the situation found in small children, usually below the age of 5 years, but sometimes as late as 11 to 12 years. Theirs is mainly a speech problem. Young children often attach little importance to their disfluency; they may not be aware that there is anything wrong. If they are aware, they may not be either concerned or worried because speech is not an issue for them. The speech problem is mostly of a simple nature because it is above the surface and out in the open.

Figure 5.2 illustrates the situation for an older child, teenager or adult. The speech symptoms, that is, the disfluency on the surface may be more frequent or more severe but, more importantly, the hidden area beneath the surface is now much more significant.

For example, take Liz. Liz is sixteen years old. She has experienced much social displeasure and negative reactions to her stammering. She has been told that she stammers, asked to take a deep breath and try again. She has been teased and has experienced difficulty in answering to her name in class and in reading out loud. All these experiences, over a period of time, have made her realise that stammering is not the best thing that could have happened to her!

She may now have feelings of worry, anxiety, embarrassment or anger but these feelings will be hidden inside her – the submerged part of the iceberg. How this effects her will depend on her personality and the help she was given in the early years. However, the more afraid, angry or depressed she becomes, the more she is likely to stammer so that she is caught in a vicious circle.

## Questions which are often asked

### Is stammering more common in boys than in girls?

Yes, there does seem to be a greater number of boys who stammer, and the ratios quoted range between three and six boys to one girl (Kidd, Kidd and Records, 1978).

### Can a child gradually or suddenly become fluent?

Yes. Many children, even when the symptoms are quite severe, can stop being disfluent as quickly as they started, or they may gradually acquire the skills of fluency as they become more competent in other areas of their development (Andrews and Harris, 1964).

### Why do some children speak well on one day and then become very hesitant the next day?

Periods of disfluency are quite normal and can be associated, for example, with excitement, fatigue or uncertainty. Stammering is a fluctuating condition so that children can be fluent for days or weeks and then suddenly become disfluent again (Walle, 1976).

### *Does the stammering child differ from the fluent child?*

It is not possible to state specific ways in which all children who stammer differ from those who are fluent. It is not possible to say that all children who stammer do not differ psychologically or physically from those who are fluent. Stammering is not a single simple disorder, so that there are considerable variations in the children who stammer as well as in the speech symptoms that they display. The old idea that, children who stammer, are timid, shy, withdrawn and nervous has been found not to be true. There are indeed timid and nervous children who stammer, just as there are timid and nervous children who do not stammer; there are also confident and outgoing children who stammer, just as there are such children who are fluent. Many questions remain unanswered regarding stammering children, but research does indicate that children who stammer may have more language and articulatory difficulties than fluent children; that more stammering children than fluent children may have anxious or demanding parents, and that there is a greater likelihood of stammering when there are relatives who stammer (Bloodstein, 1981).

## How can you help the young disfluent child

### *Some do's and don'ts*

DON'T tell children to stop stammering or to talk more slowly – if they could they would. You will only cause confusion because they do not know how to stop. They may have only a vague notion of what a stammer is.

DO remain calm and patient – if children are made fearful or tense, they may stammer more.

DO let children speak for themselves. If you speak for them or answer questions on their behalf, this will underline their inability to speak as efficiently and fluently as you do. They may feel more awkward when they have to speak for themselves.

DON'T say 'speak slowly, 'take a deep breath' or 'think before you speak'. This may sound like a criticism of their speech and may increase their awareness of their own speech in a negative way.

DO behave in the same way with stammering children as with fluent ones. For example: A nursery teacher once said, 'It's all very well telling us these things, and they make sense, but in a room full of children with varying needs, it's difficult to know what to do for the best. For instance, I have a little boy called Billy in my group and two or three times a day he rushes up to me, wiggles about and looks agonised, and then says, 'Please can I go to the t.t.t.t.' and then he gets stuck.'

'What did you do?'
'I sent him off to the toilet, but I wasn't sure whether that was the right thing to do.'

This situation was discussed amongst a group of Nursery Nurses and Teachers. It was decided that Billy was getting a reward for his behaviour and that he was being treated differently because of his speech. Had he been fluent, he would have been told to come and ask for the toilet in good time and not at the last moment. The advice given to the teacher by the group was to react quite normally the next time Billy approached her in this way and wait calmly for him to finish the word.

Some weeks later the nursery teacher reported that she had implemented the advice given and, on the first occasion, Billy looked amazed as he waited for her to send him to the toilet. Bravely, she stood her ground whilst he danced around. Finally, Billy started again and said, 'Please can I go to the t..t..t..toilet?' This teacher was well aware that Billy might have an accident, but she was no longer treating Billy differently from the other children.

DON'T interrupt the child too much. We all have difficulty remembering what we are trying to say if we are constantly interrupted. A stammering child may become confused and give up speaking, or become much more disfluent.

DON'T call children 'stammerers' or label their speech as 'stammering'. We cannot give a guarantee that a child will grow into a confirmed stammerer as s/he matures, so it is unnecessary to attach the stammering label. Once labelled, children may begin to accept the adults' evaluation and doubt their own abilities, and this may affect their performance. It may then not be clear whether the poor performance was due to a real difficulty, or due to anxiety caused by the label.

DO be a good speech model for children to copy as they will tend to speak as they are spoken to. Aim to keep your own speech calm and simple. Often our messages are too complicated for children to understand.

For example: 'Hurry up now and tidy up your table, then make sure the guinea pig has got water for the night, and get your coat because it is nearly going home time and we do not want to keep everyone waiting.'

Small children, especially disfluent ones, cannot cope with this barrage of instructions and information. Try to confine yourself to one or two simple instructions at a time.

DO reassure children who show real distress when they cannot say a word that, at times, everyone has difficulty with what they want to say. If adults accept a child's difficulties, so will the child. If the adults display concern and anxiety, so will the child.

DO try to comment on general behaviour rather than commenting specifically on speech. Explain that: 'There's no need to rush, there's plenty of time;' or distract the child's attention to a game or a task that is enjoyable.

DO react in the same way whether children are fluent or stammering. React to *what* they say and not to *how* they are saying it.

DO look for the things that the child can achieve and give plenty of praise.

Many highly successful people have stammered (Newark, 1978), including Winston Churchill, Jonathan Miller, Lewis Carol and Marilyn Monroe. The tall and the short, the fat and the thin, the beautiful and the not so beautiful, the fluent and the stammering – all can become successful providing they retain their self-confidence and self-esteem. No one is perfect, but when someone loses their self-confidence then every flaw becomes a major disaster. The more children are helped in these early years to build their confidence and self-esteem as whole human beings, and not on the basis of their fluent or disfluent speech, the more likely they are to get over the disfluent phase and, if this is impossible, to build a successful life without carrying the unnecessary burden of constant self-doubt and anxiety.

# CHAPTER 6

## Links Between Emotional/Behavioural Problems and Communication Difficulties

Alison Wintgens

As children learn about the world and the people around them they must explore, experiment and test limits which can be a trying time for even the most patient adult. This chapter looks beyond this normal stage of behaviour, at children who are unusually difficult to manage and whose social and emotional development is giving cause for concern. It particularly considers:

- what is meant by the term 'emotional and behavioural problems';
- what sort of problems are likely;
- how common these are;
- why children with communication difficulties are especially prone;
- when and why some children have these problems;
- what can be done to help.

### 'Emotional and behavioural problems' – what does this mean?

Some stages in a child's early years are likely to be more demanding on the parents or carers than others – normal young toddlers can cling anxiously, older toddlers are often said to be 'into everything' and adults may resign themselves to the fact that, 'it's the terrible twos'. Other adults may not have bargained for how lively many ordinary children are and insist that they are 'hyperactive' when they are showing normally energetic behaviour. In these examples the parents may need support and reassurance to help them through this stage if they are finding it difficult;

but it is not helpful to call it an emotional or behavioural problem in the clinical sense since it will be shown by normal children.

Clinically significant problems are more extensive or severe than behaviours or emotional reactions shown by normal children; and they interfere with children's ordinary lives and development, or cause them considerable suffering. They are the sort of problems where it may be helpful to seek specialist help.

Therefore, when an adult feels that a child behaves in a way which causes concern, it is important to look at just how severe and extensive this behaviour is. Examples of the kinds of questions which might be asked are listed below under, 'How Can You Help?' Broadly speaking, the degree of severity and its impact on the child will indicate whether this really is a clinically significant problem, and give an idea of how to help and who might help.

## What types of problems may occur?

Most people notice a child who is difficult to manage, who challenges adults, or behaves in an anti-social way; their names can become infamous and even other young children may notice and go home with tales of what 'Mary' or 'David' did today! There are also those who are quieter and less obvious, but may be in just as much need of help; the child who seems withdrawn, depressed, immature or to be behaving in an odd or puzzling way.

There are various ways of classifying the problems commonly found in the 0–7 age group. The simplest is to identify two major divisions:

### Behavioural problems

These might include:

*Feeding* – such as refusing food which may lead to failure to thrive (failing to grow and gain weight) or pica (eating inappropriate objects) – for example, the child who eats very little and whose weight is very low, or one who eats (for example) worms and insects.

*Sleeping* – taking a long time to get off to sleep, or waking at night.

*Toilet training* – wetting (also known as enuresis) or soiling (encopresis) beyond the age at which a child should be dry and clean.

*Activity* – an increased level of activity commonly coupled with a lack of concentration.

*Challenging parental control* – especially around discipline, such as at bed-times, meal times, or on trips out.

*Aggression* – excessive tantrums which may be verbal or physical, including behaviour such as hitting, scratching, biting, or deliberately destructive behaviour.

### Emotional problems

*Anxiety* – such as problems of separation from the mother, or persistent irrational fears like imagining there is a monster under the bed.

*Depression* – a miserable appearance, or excessive crying.

Such difficulties are common. Various surveys (Richman, Stevenson and Graham, 1982; Rutter, Cox, Tupling, Berger and Yule, 1975) suggest that between one in twenty and one in ten children have a clinically significant emotional and/or behavioural problem at some stage in their childhood, children from inner city areas being the most vulnerable.

## Why children with communication problems are particularly prone to emotional and behavioural problems

The link between emotional and behavioural problems and speech and language problems is strong and complex. It is easy to see a number of connections:

a) children with comprehension problems may not do what they are told because they do not understand, and thus get into trouble;

b) children who cannot make themselves understood because of unclear speech or limited expressive language may withdraw, or get so frustrated they have frequent temper tantrums;

c) children who are withdrawn do not spend as much time practising talking to others as sociable children do, and so may have delayed language development;

d) children who have suffered a traumatic shock, such as the loss of a parent or being sexually abused, may stop speaking entirely or stop speaking to adults or strangers.

In these simple examples it seems possible to see cause and effect. In the examples (a) and (b) above, there is a **Primary Communication Problem**. In examples (c) and (d) there is a Secondary **Communication Problem**.

However, the position may become increasingly complex, like a vicious circle, with both aspects closely interwoven, and it is easy to lose sight of what is primary and what is secondary.

Some experts (Prizant, Audet, Burke, Hummer, Maher and Theadore, 1990) have suggested four other ways in which emotional and behavioural problems, and speech and language are related:

1. they can co-occur, with or without obvious ties, as in the child with delayed language and depression where the two may be linked. Another child with delayed language may have sleeping problems, but these two may be unconnected;
2. the communication problem can be an essential part of the diagnosis, as in autism;
3. the communication problem can be an associated part of the diagnosis, as in learning disability;
4. the communication problem can be the sole part of the diagnosis, as in stammering. (See Chapter 5).

## Why does it happen?

It is known (Hall, Hill and Elliman, 1990) that the commonest causes of emotional and behavioural problems in early childhood are 'poor parenting', poor relationships between the child and other family members, unhelpful parental attitudes and practices, and 'deviant family functioning.' However, it is important to stress that there are many children who do not fall into these categories.

In addition, most experts would agree that it is unusual to find a single clear-cut cause for a child's emotional and/or behavioural problem. As well as interactions between the child and family there is the child's interactions with the wider environment, and, factors which are present within the child.

It may be helpful to plot possible causes on a grid such as Figure 6.1 below.

|  | Child | Family | Wider Environment |
|---|---|---|---|
| Predisposing | D | C | |
| Precipitating | | | A, B |
| Perpetuating | | | E |

**Figure 6.1** Causes of Emotional/Behavioural Problems

Predisposing factors are: any things in the past which affect the child's behaviour or emotional state. Precipitating causes occur immediately before the behaviour is noticed. Perpetuating factors are those which seem to maintain the behaviour which is causing concern.

Imagine a little boy who appears to be miserable and withdrawn following the death of his guinea-pig three months previously. This is shown as A in Figure 6.1. The death of the guinea pig is a precipitating factor. However, several other relevant causes come to light with careful questioning:

B – the child is being bullied at school, (precipitating factor);
C – his maternal grandmother died nine months ago, and his mother finds it hard to talk about death, (predisposing factor);
D – he has always had a rather introverted temperament, (predisposing factor);
E – the death of the replacement guinea-pig, (perpetuating factor).

Understanding all the various causes is essential in order to know how to help. Knowing about the grandmother's death; knowing the child's temperament; counselling for the mother; strategies to manage the bullying, and even the choice of a different or healthier pet in the future may all play a part.

Let us look at the three headings in Figure 6.1 in more detail.

### The family

One could imagine that a child with an emotional and/or behavioural problem may come from a family whose lifestyle appears chaotic, rigid, or harsh, or from a family who is considered to be deprived. Certainly the family environment, the quality of close relationships, and parental attitudes are very important to developing children. They have to move from complete dependence to independence, and for this to happen there needs to be a gradual transfer of responsibility from the adults to the children. Children's backgrounds should therefore be secure, stable, stimulating and reasonably consistent. They will be at risk of emotional and/or behavioural problems if the family relationships or members are very disturbed, or there are a lot of changes or stresses.

Going back a generation, a lot can depend on what experiences the parents themselves had as children. Unfortunately, all too often, it may be that their own family relationships were disturbed, and that possibly the pattern is being repeated. Sometimes parents make a big effort to avoid what they see as their parents' mistakes, but with no model to go by they may swing to the opposite extreme, or be inconsistent.

### The child

The child may have been born with a serious primary condition such as autism, or learning disability where the emotional and/or behavioural problems may be part of the condition.

There may be a physical problem such as cerebral palsy, deafness, or epilepsy, or an injury such as severe burns, all of which may restrict the child physically or socially, or arouse unhelpful attitudes from family or friends.

Temperamental factors may be significant. The child may not be placid and adaptable but have characteristics more vulnerable to stress or change.

### The wider environment

This area covers all other people, places or activities with which the child is involved. Events or relationships at school, nursery, or playgroup may be the cause of difficulty or distress for the child. Frequent changes of teacher, going to stay with a friend, or bullying are all examples in this category.

### Child abuse

It is important to mention child abuse here, although it does need to be regarded separately. Using Figure 6.1 it could be plotted under 'Family' or 'Wider Environment', depending on who the abuser was or is. The time of the abuse will influence whether it is plotted as a predisposing, precipitating or perpetuating factor.

The term 'child abuse' is used when the quality of care and protection of children is thought, by current standards, to be so poor that children may be said to have been abused. Incidents of child abuse are becoming increasingly well known and may be partly or wholly the cause of a child's emotional and/or behavioural problem. Although many children suffer several forms of abuse, there are four main types:

1. physical, or non-accidental injury (NAI), where children are physically injured or damaged not as the result of an accident;

2. emotional, where parents so threaten or verbally abuse children that they become very fearful;

3. neglect, where parents fail to protect children or to provide an adequate environment for their development;

4. sexual (also known as CSA – child sex abuse) when sexually mature people involve children in any sexual activity.

## How can you help children with emotional/behavioural problems?

### Documenting the problem and understanding how and why it occurs

1. Watch the child carefully and see, as exactly as possible, what the problem is, how, when and with whom it happens and how often.

It is easy, for example, to turn round and see Ben hitting Louise. But this could have happened in a number of ways, such as: a seemingly unprovoked attack; tit-for-tat paying back which Louise started; or, Ben's attempt to defend his younger sister whom Louise just accidentally knocked over.

Close observations make it much easier to describe a problem, deal with it, and to tell if it is getting better or worse. It may be helpful to describe the behaviour bearing in mind a simplified version of the 'ABC'. This ABC method is a part of 'Behaviour Modification', (Herbert, 1987) a way of treating children's behaviour problems which is frequently used by psychologists.

A are the Antecedents, or what came immediately before the incident, what exactly the child and relevant others were doing. B is the Behaviour itself – what exactly the child does, the place, time, situation and people involved. C are the Consequences, what exactly other people do or say as a result of the behaviour.

2. Get a description of the 'problem' from all angles by talking to others involved with the child – parents, other close family members, teachers, nursery nurses, therapists or other carers. Ask the following questions:

- what exactly happens?
- with whom does the 'problem' exist?
- to what extent does it affect different aspects of the child's and family's lives?
- is the child's development affected?

3. Find out how concerned other people are. You might ask:

- who is most worried?
- how worried are they?

This will give you an idea of the severity of the problem; whether you should turn to specialists for help, and how motivated the parents are to change things.

4.   Ask what people have done to try and solve the problem. Ask, 'What do you do when Matthew won't eat?' or '... when Vanessa screams?' Get an idea of various solutions people have attempted and how well they have worked. In this way you may not only get an idea of a new and helpful solution, but also a chance to see how consistently the problem is handled.

### Using simple management tactics

Difficult behaviour often happens quickly and needs to be dealt with immediately. There may be little time to think out the best solution and your reaction to it might be almost a reflex. Nevertheless, here are a few principles and suggestions for managing, along with a warning that the behaviour may seem to get worse at first if you change your way of dealing with it, but in the long-term there will be definite improvements and benefits.

- Ignore when (and if!) possible.
- Divert and distract especially if the child is younger, or if you catch a situation early enough and anticipate trouble ahead.
- Set clear limits and stick to them – for example, if you ask a child to put away some toys, see it through, even if you have to give a lot of encouragement, or a little help.
- Choose only the most important things to correct – if you constantly tell a child off it loses its effect.
- Explain briefly why you are telling a child to do (or not to do) something – 'because I say so,' teaches them nothing.
- Make explanations and instructions short and simple, especially if the child is quite young, or may have a language problem.
- Be specific – tell him/her exactly what you want rather than a vague instruction to, 'be a good boy/girl.'
- Tell (instruct), don't ask, if you want something done – 'Are you going to pick that up?' invites the answer, 'No!'
- Give clear messages – for example if you say, 'No, don't do that,' make sure your face is serious with no hint of laughing.

- Show that you are pleased (with praise, smiles, hugs or whatever) when the child is behaving and has done what was asked (maybe picked up something that was thrown, or said sorry to someone).
- Use your voice, face and body to reinforce the message you want to get across.
- Find out and talk about the feelings that are underlying the behaviour, so the child learns that the feelings are acceptable but the behaviour is not. For example, you might say, 'I know you're feeling cross because we can't go to the park, but you're not to (deliberately) spill your drink.'
- Think the best of children and try and see it their way – if they do not do what they are told try and think why, rather than assume they are disobedient; there may be a conflict of interests or a lack of understanding, rather than a deliberate attempt to provoke.
- Try to keep as calm as possible – if a child is deliberately trying to annoy you, don't rise to the bait!

The following suggestions may come in useful with children who are shy or withdrawn, very active, or lacking in motivation.

- Try and get very active children to stick at a task for just half a minute more, or to look at just one more page of a book. Build it up gradually rather than be unrealistic and expect them to concentrate for quarter of an hour, or finish a whole book.
- If children won't pay attention or play with what you want them to, get involved in what they are doing and try and adapt that for your purposes. Start where the child is and gradually help them tolerate adult involvement, or gradually move away to your choice of task.
- Don't pay extra attention to shy children – it only makes it worse. Leave them to join in or speak in their own time, and give plenty of reassurance.
- Interesting or adult-like equipment can help with a child who has poor attention or concentration – for example, a calculator instead of dice to encourage a 7 year old to try a board game; or a bull-dog type clip for a pre-school child to use to hold pictures or cards.
- With children with poor talking and/or low self-esteem, respond and give encouragement for the smallest thing they contribute, and watch for their nonverbal attempts as well.
- Prepare children for change, whether it is a change of routine, a new significant adult in their lives, or a different arrangement of a familiar room. Many children (and adults) find change difficult especially if

they are emotionally vulnerable, so give warning and involve children in preparations for change.

### Helping parents

1. *Don't just give bad news.* If you need to talk to parents about something that bothers you – perhaps the child never joins in group activities, seems to be a loner and has poor concentration – it is usually helpful to talk about how the child is getting on in general. That way there is a chance for the parents to hear some good news about the child as well as what you are worried about.

2. *Work in partnership with the parents,* sharing information and discussing solutions or changes. They know the child best and are the ones who have to live with him and have to find a way of managing him which works and with which they are happy. (See Chapter 10).

3. *Find a common language.* If parents say, 'It's her moods that worry us,' make sure that you, they, and the child, if she is old enough, all know exactly what is meant by the word 'moods'; for example, 'When she puts on a sulky face, sits doing nothing and won't talk to anyone.

4. *Avoid blaming either parent or child.* The chances are that the problem is in the way in which one particular child interacts with one or both parent(s), together with a combination of several causes as was discussed earlier. With that in mind you can avoid blame and guilt which are not helpful in solving the problem.

5. *Support parents and boost their confidence.* Remember that it can be miserable for parents if their child does not behave in an acceptable way and may lead to a feeling of guilt and failure. Praise what is going well, and encourage the parents.

6. *Try and find a solution which the parents are trying, or want to try.* Parents often do have the answers, but sometimes they lack confidence or staying power. Maybe they have been undermined by someone from the generation above who has stepped in to try and help; or maybe they feel that what they try never seems to work, although it may well do if they stick to one thing and see it through consistently.

### Referral for further help

If you and/or the family have tried to manage the problem yourselves and are still worried you should look for outside help.

Several specialists are available to advise on children's emotional and behavioural problems. Who you turn to may depend on the setting the child is in (for example, nursery, clinic or school) or where the family lives.

The most obvious specialists are:

– clinical psychologist
– educational psychologist – generally if the child is at school
– child psychiatrist – especially if the problem is severe and persistent.

Referrals are usually made via the school, health visitor, community doctor, therapist or GP.

Before referring, many specialists welcome a telephone call to discuss whether they are the most suitable person/team to turn to. A referral letter with a good description of the problem is necessary, and sometimes the referrer is invited to the first appointment so that all concerns can be discussed openly with the family. For any treatment to be effective, it is important that parents recognise the difficulties, and want to change them themselves, not just to keep the nursery, the social worker or whoever quiet.

## Conclusion

Emotional and behavioural problems should always be taken seriously. Many of them are surprisingly persistent and it cannot be assumed that reassurance and the attitude that a child will always 'grow out of it', will be enough. Even common problems, like waking at night, can be very draining on a family.

Nevertheless, facing up to these problems and working with the children and their families is very worthwhile. Understanding children's emotional and social development and their behaviour, as well as normal family functioning, are fascinating areas of study. The improvements which can be seen as a result of successful management have enormous benefits for the child and family.

# CHAPTER 7

# *The Role of the Speech and Language Therapist*

## Jannet A. Wright

Speech and language therapists are the professionals who are contacted if a child is known to have a speech and language problem or if parents and/or teachers are concerned about the way in which a child communicates.

In the UK the majority of speech and language therapists are employed by the National Health Service, although they may work in nurseries, language units, special and mainstream schools, as well as health centres and hospitals. Some therapists specialise and work solely in a school for the deaf or physically disabled children, or children with learning disabilities.

Another area of specialisation may be working with children from bilingual backgrounds who are having difficulties learning the language spoken at home as well as English. They will not be seen by a therapist unless they are having problems in both their first language and English. The therapist will need to ascertain the level of the child's difficulties in the first language by gathering information from the parents and the child, often using interpreters. If children have a problem in their first language as well as in learning English, then the speech and language therapist will work with the families to help the children develop the underlying skills necessary for language learning.

As stated in Chapter 2, communication begins at birth, so therapists may be asked to see children from birth onwards. Therapists may become involved with children and their families very early in the children's development. This may be to help with communication or if there are any feeding problems such as those associated with a cleft palate or a physical problem that has been identified at birth.

A speech and language therapist investigates a child's abilities as well as the difficulties they may be having with communication. The child will be looked at individually. The therapist will also consider the patterns of interaction in the family. This enables the therapist to identify the problems that the child is having with communication as well as looking at any features in the child's environment which may be contributing to these difficulties. The therapist will discuss with the parents their child's communication and work out with them the best way to help their child.

If the child attends a school or a nursery the therapist will, with the parents' permission, talk to the teachers about how the child communicates with the staff as well as with other children. In this situation the therapist will want to work with both the teachers and the parents to help the child. It is also important for the therapist to ensure that ideas for therapy which may arise from the speech and language assessment can be integrated with the curriculum topics and teaching methods used in the school.

## Referral to speech and language therapy

Speech and language therapists will usually have a base for administrative purposes and where messages may be left for them, although they may work in several different places during each week.

Children may be referred to a speech and language therapist by their parents. Other sources of referral include the GP, health visitors, teachers or any other concerned professional. The professional who refers a child to speech and language therapy will hopefully have explained to the parents the reason for such a referral. A speech and language therapist cannot see a child unless the parents have given their permission.

## Service delivery

The local arrangements for speech and language therapy service provision are influenced by the demands of the National Health Service, the local education authority and the schools. This means that the organisation of services will vary from one geographical area to another. Thus, for example, a child with a communication problem who lives in Doncaster may come into contact with a service organised in a different way from a child with the same problem who lives in Cornwall.

## Clinic based services

Even within one geographical area speech and language therapists may vary the frequency of the speech and language therapy appointments that they offer. This will depend on the needs of the child, the family's commitments, the therapist's rationale for the management of that child and the organisation of the local services. Therapists may offer a weekly appointment or one every month or six weeks. The length of time that children and their families spend with a therapist will vary, depending on the needs of the children. Sometimes an appointment will last 30 to 45 minutes, whereas some appointments may last up to one and a half hours. If an individual child is seen as part of a group then they may be asked to attend for a whole morning or an afternoon.

Usually at least one parent accompanies the child and joins in the therapy so that the work the speech and language therapist does with the child can be continued on a daily basis. During the session there may be time to encourage parents to practise certain activities in order that these may then be continued at home. Parents need to be involved as much as possible from the time of referral to speech and language therapy.

Intensive courses may be offered during the school holidays. Children attend such courses on a daily basis in the summer or at Easter and parents may also be asked to attend.

## School based services

If a child attends a special school a speech and language therapist may be based there. Children attending mainstream schools may go to the local health centre for speech and language therapy appointments, although this may mean that they have to take time off school. In an increasing number of areas speech and language therapists are working within mainstream schools where they liaise directly with the teachers. Each therapist has to negotiate where to see the child and when. The teacher and therapist will discuss the effect the communication problem has on the child's academic work and how therapy may be incorporated into curricular activities.

Some of the children seen by a speech and language therapist may have a Statement of Special Educational Need to which the therapist may have contributed a report. The provision of speech and language therapy may be either the main need of the child or one of many. In some statements the provision of speech and language therapy is included in the educational section but in others it is included as a provision under health.

## What will the Speech and Language Therapist do?

The therapist will need to ask the parents about their child's development and health in order to see if there are any links between the communication problems and general development. The therapist will also be interested in who referred the child and why, so that the problem can be seen through the eyes of the adult who made the referral.

The speech and language therapist will want to know the results of the child's latest hearing test. In some cases this may involve arranging further assessments before therapy can begin. This is to establish whether the child's problems are related to any hearing difficulties.

## Assessment

The speech and language therapist needs to obtain a complete picture of the child, including speech and language skills.

The assessment of communication problems involves using materials with which children are comfortable, namely toys. The way in which they play can reveal a great deal about the way in which they think and understand the world around them and aspects of their intellectual functioning. The therapist will also be interested in the children's attention, how long they play with one toy, their interaction skills and their nonverbal communication such as gestures, pointing and eye contact.

The child's language development will be discussed with the parents. Therapists need to know how children speak, what they understand and what they talk about. The way in which children relate to other people will also be of interest.

### Understanding

The therapist will try to work out how much a child understands, using a variety of assessment techniques. It may appear that children 'understand everything that is said to them' but if situational clues are removed they may have more difficulty. Formal tests may be used to reduce the clues which children can utilise and scores on a particular test may be converted into 'age equivalent' scores so that the performance of children of a similar age can be compared.

*Expression*

During the speech and language therapy session the therapist may, with the parents' agreement, use a tape recorder to collect examples of children's language. These language samples will be analysed by the therapist after the session. They can then be considered in detail and compared to developmental norms in order to identify children's communication strengths and weaknesses. The therapist will note the grammatical structures as well as the vocabulary that children use.

*Speech sounds*

While therapists analyse these language samples they also listen to the speech sounds the children use. If this is an area of particular concern therapists will ask children to name some pre-selected pictures which will provide examples of pronunciation of a wide range of sounds. The therapist will study the production of single words and words in continuous speech, as in the language sample, to see if there is a pattern in the way certain sounds are produced, omitted or substituted. Again the therapist will compare each child's speech to known developmental patterns in order to plan therapy.

*Team assessment*

Sometimes the speech and language therapist works with other professionals such as paediatricians, psychologists and teachers in order to gain a complete picture of the child. A group of professionals may form a team which comes together as required by the needs of an individual child; or the team may be one which works together consistently and is for example based in a hospital or child development centre. In the latter case this may help to reduce the number of hospital appointments a family has to attend and parents may see the therapist at the same time as other professionals.

## Integrating Speech and Language Therapy

A speech and language therapy session either once a week or even daily during term time will only be successful if the therapy is integrated into a child's life style.

If speech and language therapy is offered in a school setting the therapist faces the same issues which arise for other support services. These include decisions about seeing the child in the classroom, taking them out into another room for therapy and arranging time to talk to the teacher. All these negotiations are potentially time consuming but necessary if a child is to receive a co-ordinated programme of intervention from therapists and teachers. Only with such co-ordination will children with speech and language problems receive the consistent support which will enable them to integrate their newly acquired skills into their everyday lives.

# CHAPTER 8

# *Language Programmes*

## Myra Kersner

The term **Language Programme** is frequently used by professionals involved in working with children with communication difficulties, and yet it may be used in a different way by each professional. It may refer to various methods of approach.

For example, there are **Informal Individual Language Programmes**, speech and language work-schedules designed for individual children; or there are more **Formalised Programmes**, such as unpublished 'locally used' programmes; or formalised programmes which may have been published as books, 'Language Kits', or video courses (Harris, 1984).

In fact the term 'Language Programme' may refer to any structured framework which has been devised for the specific purpose of encouraging speech, and teaching language, based on the careful assessment of individual children.

## Types of programme

### *Informal individual language programmes*

It is important that, wherever possible, language teaching and learning should not be seen as a separate 'lesson'. Some of the most effective language programmes are based on teaching which is structured, but which occurs in a naturalistic setting. That is, the programme is designed so that language may be taught at every available opportunity, as a natural part of the child's everyday life (see Chapter 9). Following assessment, programmes may be devised for individual children, so that appropriate words can be emphasised, sentences modelled and expanded, or new vocabulary taught, whilst games are being played at home or at school; while carrying out ordinary household functions, such as cooking or cleaning; or as part of regular classroom activities. However, in addition to this informal approach, it may help some children to spend some 'special' time concentrating on language. For these extra sessions, more formalised Language Programmes may prove useful.

### Unpublished locally used programmes

Many speech and language therapists, specialist language teachers or psychologists devise their own language programmes based on their knowledge and understanding of speech and language development, and their practical experiences of assessing and working with children with communication problems. These programmes may be used locally within a school, or more widely throughout a district or region.

### Books

Sometimes these programmes may be written up as part of a book which is then published and made available to a wider readership. Examples of these are: *Working with Children's Language* (Cooke and Williams, 1985); *Let Me Speak* (Jeffrie and McConkey, 1976); *Let's Play* (McConkey and Gallagher, 1984); *Learning Language and Loving it* (Weitzman, 1992), or *Talking Together* (Hall, 1990).

### Language kits

Some programmes are published as complete packages with full instructions and manuals, such as *Living Language* (Locke, 1985); *Teaching Talking* (Locke and Beech, 1991); *The Hanen Early Language Parent Programme* (1985) or *The Derbyshire Language Scheme* (Knowles and Masidlover, 1982) which require the users to undergo specialist training.

### Video cassettes

Some of the programmes mentioned above are to be found on a video cassette, specifically structured for teaching and training purposes. Examples of these are the videos regarding the use of *Living Language*, *Learning Language and Loving It*, or other aspects of the Hanen Programme.

## Which type of programme to choose

There are many features which need to be considered when deciding which of the published programmes to use. Several questions need to be asked, such as: what population of children was it designed for? What is the range of language features covered? How much expert knowledge is required in order to carry it out? Can it be used with individuals as well as groups? (Harris, 1990). It is important to be aware of each programme's individual advantages as well as its limitations. It is always advisable to choose and implement a programme in collaboration with a speech and language specialist, to ensure that the most appropriate choice is made, in order that each child might gain maximum benefit.

One criticism which is often levelled against published language programmes is their rigidity of structure and lack of flexibility. However, this need not be the case. If the theoretical principles on which the programme is based are understood, it may often be possible to adapt the programme, within the structure provided, to meet individual children's needs. Indeed, most of the programmes include suggestions for adaptations.

Below is an outline of some of the formalised published programmes which are in frequent use.

## *Living Language* by Ann Locke

*Living Language* is designed specifically for use with children with communication difficulties who are in nurseries or mainstream schools. It is a remedial programme for teaching spoken language that can be used by anyone who spends a significant part of each day with young children. This may include teachers in special and mainstream schools, nursery nurses and nursery teachers, or parents. Procedures for assessing a child's current functioning in specific areas, plus suggestions for promoting development of weaker areas, are given in the programme.

Within the nursery it can provide a means of screening children in order to identify those who would benefit from additional help in establishing spoken language. It also offers suggestions for how to work with them. In addition, the methods outlined can be used, with modifications, to enable staff to organise classroom activities which will promote the development of spoken language in all children, and will prepare children to meet the requirements of the National Curriculum when they start school.

*Living Language* includes three separate but overlapping teaching programmes: The Pre-Language Programme, Before Words; The Starter Programme, First Words, and The Main Programme, Putting Words Together. All the relevant instructions, manuals and record forms are in a sturdy folder. Additional materials such as Picture Resource which may be used to help implement the programme, are available for purchase separately.

*The Pre-language Programme, Before Words*, is intended for use with children who have little or no understanding of language. It covers development normally shown in children from birth to two years. It provides a breakdown of those areas of a child's development that underlie the emergence of language: social-emotional development; play; listening skills; and expressive skills. Delayed or patchy development in any of these areas may contribute towards a child's slow language development and it is important to help promote these skills at the same time as language itself.

*The Starter Programme, First Words*, is intended for use with children who have begun to use language, but are still largely at a single word stage. It covers development normally shown in children from around one to three years of age. It consists of one hundred of the most basic words children need to know before they can develop more complex language.

*The Main Programme, Putting Words Together*, is intended for children who already have a basic vocabulary and are beginning to combine single words to form sentences. It gives a comprehensive breakdown of vocabulary and grammatical features of English, which children are likely to establish at some time between two and seven years of age, though the upper age limit is open-ended. These are organised in such a way that they can be 'taught', or their learning encouraged, as part of the domestic routines and teaching activities that regularly take place throughout the day.

### Planning intervention

The main principle of intervention used in *Living Language* is to provide opportunities for those activities and responses that enable all children to acquire and use language. The only significant difference is that children identified as having communication difficulties are likely to need these experiences more frequently and perhaps in a wider range of situations than children normally require. Thus, they may benefit from increased opportunities to play, especially with an adult, or they may require help in learning to listen and respond to sound, or to express themselves.

The aim of intervention with children who fail the initial screen is to help them establish those words in the Starter Programme vocabulary they do not use spontaneously. It is essential that new vocabulary is taught throughout the day in context, for it is by using words in familiar situations that children first come to see what they mean and gradually learn to use them for themselves.

*Establishing Vocabulary – Sample activities*

A selection of activities around the teaching of a particular word such as 'apple' might include:

- Visits to shops to buy apples, or a garden to pick apples.
- Cooking apple-shaped biscuits; preparing apple and banana fruit salad; making toffee apples, or baked apples.
- At breaktime, cutting up apples – where possible letting the children help.
- Eating apples, perhaps offering a choice between apples, bananas or oranges.
- Setting up a shop with different items for sale. These can be drawn from the one hundred words and can be made up by the children from playdough, plasticine or papier mache. Apples can be red/green/yellow; big/small. Other items can be included such as biscuits, milk or sweets. This activity can be made more realistic by including such items as paper bags, baskets/bags, a till and money, and a simple balance using a coat hanger and two large margarine cartons.
- The children might help to make posters of the items which are for sale.
- Making models. Draw a tree trunk on card three to four feet high and pin it to the wall. Make cardboard branches. Paint it, then, pin one end to the wall, making the branches hang away from wall. Make three-dimensional apples, for example using clear tights which have been stuffed and painted, and put them on the tree. Adding drops of apple oil, or a similar oil, will give the apples an nice smell for the children to sniff.
- Making 'musical mats' in the shape of apples. The children stand on an apple when the music stops.
- Printing with apple shapes can make up designs, for example, on wrapping paper. This could then be used to wrap a small gift to take home.

- Drawing and cutting out pictures which illustrate apples. These can then be mounted on cardboard and cut into two, three or four pieces to make jigsaw puzzles.

These activities could be extended to any other word in the core vocabulary. By using one word as a focus for activities in this way, many other words will be used regularly, enabling children to learn them in context and at their own pace.

## Promoting talk in the nursery classroom

Adult involvement in activities provides a vital source of regular conversation for children, for, although young children do talk to each other, the majority of nursery aged children need to hear adults talking to them regularly to help them extend their vocabulary and use language in an increasing range of ways. Young children should be encouraged to extend their learning about themselves and other people, their home and immediate neighbourhood, and to extend their exploration of the physical world of plants and animals. This aspect of early education can be helped by taking a theme that is likely to be of interest and value to children, and using it as a means of extending their knowledge at the same time as promoting skills.

Learning about 'Myself' is a common example of such a theme in nurseries and schools. It is invaluable then if all members of staff contribute to the development of a 'thematic web'. Activities might include:

- discussion of 'what we do with our hands/arms/legs/feet' in PE and songs;
- making drawings, paintings and models of 'Myself'.

The Main Programme of *Living Language* provides a wide range of such topics or themes, and suggests specific vocabulary that can be promoted with each one. As with the Starter Programme vocabulary, the teaching method used reflects normal language learning, with adults talking regularly to children in the course of familiar and interesting activities. By making sure that selected items of vocabulary are repeated regularly, adults will be able to provide the repetition needed to enable children to understand these words and eventually use them spontaneously.

## *Teaching Talking* by Ann Locke and Maggie Beech

*Teaching Talking* was designed in order to help professionals identify and work with children, at nursery or primary level, who are experiencing difficulties with communication. It enables teachers to fulfil the requirements of the Code of Practice for schools by being able to adjust their classroom practice in order to meet the needs of such children. The philosophy of the approach is to provide practical teaching methods to enable children's language skills to develop and be consolidated. Detailed suggestions are given as to how this support and help may be given using the materials and routines already in place in the nursery or school, and within the core subjects of the National Curriculum.

### Assessment

The Initial Screening section of the programme encourages specific observation of the children in their communicative interactions with other children and with adults over a period of time. This allows teachers to identify children who are experiencing difficulties. Practical suggestions are offered for ways in which children may be helped at this stage, for example by helping them to communicate more effectively with their peers. Children's social-emotional development, intellectual development, and skills and abilities in listening and talking can then be charted on The Pre-Language Record (for children aged two and under) and The Emerging Language Record (for children between two and five).

This will then enable the teacher to plan a programme to encourage the development of an individual child's communication skills, and/or to refer that child for specific help as required, such as a hearing test.

### Planned activities

Most importantly, children need repetition and the chance to practise their developing language skills within familiar settings. *Teaching Talking* is designed so that activities can be built into general classroom activities. Teaching suggestions are offered in the Teaching Resources Handbook regarding the development of listening and understanding, playing, relating and talking to other children so that they may all become part of the child's daily routine. Physical activities are recommended so that language is associated with active play, as well as real life activities.

*Evaluation*

The programme includes regular evaluation of the children so that their progress may be noted, and further assessment and help be offered to those who continue to experience difficulties.

In such instances, a more detailed profile may be obtained through charting of the child's progress in: physical skills; self-help and independence skills; hand-eye co-ordination; play and social development; listening and understanding, and expressive skills. 'Teaching objectives are set to consolidate children's learning where they have already begun to make some progress,' (Locke, 1994), and the programme offers detailed suggestions as to how teachers may focus on specific objectives to help improve the child's language skills.

*Further assessment and intervention*

The third stage of assessment and intervention enables teachers to monitor children who are continuing to experience difficulties. Their language skills may then be assessed further, using the second stage of the programme, and appropriate additional intervention planned.

At each of the stages there is a resources handbook offering suggestions and containing activities which may be included in the programme.

## *The Derbyshire Language Scheme* (DLS) by Wendy Knowles and Mark Masidlover

This scheme, also encourages its users to be flexible, imaginative and innovative in their use of the material provided. It is a resource pack of assessment and teaching materials which was designed by a psychologist and a teacher to help teachers provide greater language learning opportunities for the children in their classroom. It has been found to be useful for all children with speech and language difficulties, and 'extends beyond teaching sessions to the child's normal environment' (Masidlover, 1994).

The scheme underlines the fact that there is a two-way flow to communication. It is based on the premise that 'effective intervention needs to be based on an accurate knowledge of the child's existing abilities,' (Harris, 1984). For this reason it contains assessment procedures for teachers and/or therapists to assess the children's comprehension and expressive language levels, so that it will become clear at what level help should be given. The teaching activities are linked to this assessment and cover the communication skills which normally develop in children between the ages of eight months and five years. The skills are usually taught in the approximate order in which they develop, and success is measured in terms of 'spontaneous use of these skills in the child's natural environment' (Masidlover, 1994). The aim is to teach language skills in a simplified context which is conducive to communication, through activities which are of interest to the child.

There are three main teaching sections which cover both comprehension and expression of language: The Single Word Level; The Two, Three and Four Word Levels; and Level Five to Ten which covers more advanced grammatical forms.

### Assessment

The level of language assessed ranges from just prior to the emergence of the understanding of single words, and progresses in logical sequence to the comprehension of the more complex aspects of grammar which are most important in early language development, such as: questions, tenses and relative clauses.

There is a *Rapid Screening Test*, which is a short test of comprehension. This is simple and quick to administer and helps to establish the level at which the more detailed comprehension assessment should be administered.

The *Detailed Comprehension Test* structures the assessment of the child's understanding across the range outlined above. It is a battery of sub-tests which also enables the assessment of Expression – see below.

In earlier chapters (Chapters 2 and 4) it has been shown how children pick up comprehension clues from the context of a situation, which help them to make sense of the words used. For example, the instruction: 'Go and wash your hands,' will usually be given when the child's hands have become particularly dirty during an activity, or prior to a mealtime; that is, at a time when the child would expect to hear such an instruction, when the situation gives additional clues to the meaning of the words. Similarly if the child is told: 'Pick up the book,' when it has just fallen to the floor.

In the DLS, the contextual clues are minimised and the child's comprehension is assessed according to the number of **Information Carrying Words** (ICWs) which need to be understood, that is the 'important' words in the sentence which the child is able to process when first hearing a simple instruction.

The vocabulary used is checked separately, to ensure that the child is familiar with the words being used. Then, limited choices are given in order to assess the child's comprehension of specific words. For example, if the child is given a set of objects: a biscuit, a brush, a doll and a teddy, the instruction is given: 'Feed dolly'; the child has to understand the two information carrying words 'feed' and 'dolly' in order to carry out this instruction.

In another example, using the same objects, if the child is asked to: 'Brush teddy'; 'teddy' and 'brush' would be the information carrying words in that sentence, as these are the words which would need to be understood in order for the instruction to be carried out correctly.

Expressive language which may be used by the child during the course of the assessment may be recorded at the same time. Although the situation is not entirely naturalistic, the child's speech used at this time should be spontaneous and natural, and will thus provide a representative sample of his/her expressive communication abilities.

This assessment process may be repeated as necessary, each re-assessment being recorded on a Progress Record Form. Thus the child's progress may be constantly evaluated.

A Class Chart enables the teacher to plot the individual levels of comprehension/expression of the children in the class. This will enable careful structuring of the levels of group activities.

*Teaching activities*

From the information gathered during the comprehension and expressive assessment teachers and/or therapists are able to ensure that new language structures and vocabulary are introduced to individual children at an appropriate level. They can utilize appropriately the teaching suggestions and activities provided in the manuals.

Initially new structures are introduced in a simplified way, their use gradually being increased and incorporated into regular classroom activities, until the goal, as expressed in the teaching manual, is reached of their: 'spontaneous, creative use in the real world.' Every opportunity is taken to encourage the child's expressive language skills within the context of the child's normal every day environment. Normal play activities may be carefully structured, and games such as hiding games used in order to encourage the child to use spoken language. The use of **role reversal** may also be helpful where the child takes on the role of 'teacher' asking questions and giving information to the rest of the class.

*The materials*

The manuals contain the assessment instructions, and teaching suggestions, although it is necessary to go on a course before these materials may be acquired or used.

The early activity suggestions are based on the use of toys and real objects. As the child's conceptual and symbolic understanding develops, pictures may be used instead. Some specific toys are often associated with this scheme, such as teddy bears, tables and chairs. However, although packages of such materials may be purchased separately from a variety of manufacturers and distributors, these are not an integral part of the materials provided. The authors strongly recommend that users are flexible in their approach, and that materials used for assessment and teaching should be appropriate to the age and interests of the individual child.

## Using parent-child interaction as an approach to helping children develop speech and language

We referred in Chapter 2 to the importance of parents' interactions with their child in facilitating language development. Several specific approaches have been developed in recent years, to help children who are experiencing language difficulties, which concentrate on this parent-child interaction for remediation. One particular method – The Hanen Approach – was developed in North America; others have been evolved from work undertaken by therapists in the UK, such as Kelman and Schneider, 1994, who work in London.

### The Hanen Approach

The Hanen programme was first implemented and developed in Canada in the 1960s for use with pre-school children. Since that time there have been many new developments, both in Canada and the UK, which have resulted in the publication of materials and training packages, all of which are based on the same principle of early intervention by parents. Such intervention is most appropriate between the ages of eighteen months and three years. The overall approach will be discussed below, and the parent training as well as one specific resource book for teachers will be referred to in more detail.

### The Hanen Early Language Parent Programme

The basic premise of this programme is that parent-child interaction skills are a prerequisite to language development (as discussed in Chapter 2). Parents' positive responses to a child's attempts to communicate enable these interaction skills to develop. In turn, well developed interaction skills offer a child increased opportunities to develop language skills.

All the materials relating to the Hanen programme are aimed at helping parents to maximise their interactions with their young children so that they may encourage and enhance language development. Parents are shown how to 'take advantage of the natural and spontaneous opportunities for communication which arise at home' (Fryer, 1994), and to develop and use the knowledge about their child which they already possess.

### The training programme

Parents (or two important people in the child's life) are invited to join a training programme. The trainers will normally include a speech and language therapist. Wherever possible, nursery/primary school teachers are advised of the meetings and are also invited to attend, so that a cooperative, holistic approach can be taken for each child.

Group sessions normally run in the evening, once a week, for a pre-arranged number of sessions (approximately ten). The advantage of group training is that parents/teachers may exchange information, as well as offer support to each other. There may be one or more home visits during the training period.

One special feature of Hanen training programmes is that the parents and child are videotaped periodically while they are interacting – playing together or talking together. These videos are viewed by the parents as well as the trainers; initially, in order to increase awareness and ultimately, in order to note progress. Opportunities are provided to enable parents to use their own experiences in order to provide a base for their new knowledge.

The parents are actively involved in all the sessions, for example they will help to formulate the objectives of the sessions and will be invited to offer feedback regarding their own and others' progress. In this way, each group is able to focus on the needs of the specific children involved, and adaptations to the programme may be made as appropriate. Adaptations may also be made according to the needs of the parents within each group, for example if there are parents for whom English is not their first language.

Helpful literature in the form of Parent Guidebooks and Handbooks is also available.

### The sessions

The overall aim of the programme is to help the parents improve the ways in which they interact with and respond to their child, and to show them the level of language that is needed so that they offer him/her the best opportunity to develop speech and language. The programme content is broken down into two modules.

In Module I the aims of the sessions are to train parents to become aware of their own responses to the communication attempts initiated by their child during the course of a day; and to improve on these responses where necessary. They are given detailed checklists so that they may become more aware of their child's ability to communicate. They are encouraged to follow their child's lead, gradually responding with comments and expanded models of sentences. They are encouraged to engage in joint activities with their children so that turn taking may be extended and improved.

In Module II, parents are encouraged to plan activities for their child which offer opportunities for interaction and dialogue, thereby enabling language development. Music, books, games and art are all explored, parents choosing their own medium and their own goals appropriate to the needs of their child. Videotaping and home visits occur during the course of sessions.

Several weeks after the initial training programme a follow-up session is usually arranged in order to discuss progress and any difficulties which may have arisen.

It is now possible to attend a course organised by a Hanen Centre in the UK (see the Appendix).

### Learning Language and Loving It – a Guide to Promoting Children's Social and Language Development in Early Childhood Settings by Elaine Weitzman

In the same way as the training programme outlined above is designed for parents, resources are available suggesting ways in which teachers may help young children once they begin to attend nursery and early infant classes. Much of the material in this book is drawn from the Hanen Language Programme for Early Childhood Educators, which has been adapted from the parent programme described above.

The aim of the book is to demonstrate to teachers – using cartoon-illustrations and examples – how they may increase the number of opportunities in which young children may interact in the classroom. As with the parents' programme, the suggestions are intended to be included as part of their every day routine, so underlining the fact that interaction and communication are natural activities. By increasing and improving the children's interactional skills, they will be providing opportunities for the improvement and continuing development of the children's language.

The book is divided into four main sections.

Part 1 offers suggestions aimed at heightening the teacher's awareness of children's need for interaction and for gathering information.

Part 2 looks at ways in which teachers may help children who are having difficulties with communication to interact actively with their peers, as well as with other adults.

Part 3 explores different avenues through which children may gather information and increase their experiences. This increased knowledge of the world will then help them to develop their inner as well as their spoken language.

Part 4 suggests ways in which teachers may promote the attitudes, skills and knowledge in children which will provide the foundation on which literacy skills may be built.

### *Other Hanen Materials*

There are videos as well as other written materials available for nursery/primary teachers and parents either from the Hanen Centre in Toronto, Canada (for further details please see the Appendix) or through Winslow Press, the publishers in Britain.

Three other books which are not specific language programmes are outlined below, as they may prove useful in encouraging the language development of young children.

### *Working with Children's Language* by Jackie Cooke and Diana Williams

This book, in its authors' words, is designed 'to stimulate language in children whose language is delayed, but who are otherwise developing normally.'

There is a brief theoretical overview included with each chapter, but essentially this is a resource book, offering ideas for ways in which pre-language development may be stimulated. For example, activities are described to improve attention skills, as well as the development of concepts and symbolic understanding.

Suggestions are offered which may promote the development of early language skills as outlined in Chapter 2. These include activities to encourage early vocalisation, babbling, and the development of first words.

The book also refers to different teaching techniques, including the role reversal which is described in the Derbyshire Language Scheme.

As stressed above, it is important that assessment to discern the appropriate level for intervention is undertaken by a speech and language specialist, but the activities outlined in this book may be used successfully, by any nursery nurse, teacher, or carer working with the children, or may be suggested to parents.

### *Let Me Speak* by Dorothy Jeffrie and Roy McConkey

This book, which is part of the Human Horizon Series, is intended for both professionals and parents 'who are interested in furthering any child's language development,' (Jeffrie and McConkey, 1976). Although first published in 1976, at the time of going to press, it was still available. The text refers to The Parent Involvement Project (PIP) directed by the authors, which resulted in the PIP Developmental Charts. These charts cover all aspects of development: Physical; Social; Eye/Hand; Play Development, and Language Development.

The book concentrates on the language development aspect of the charts, offering ways in which children's language behaviour may be documented, and suggesting activities to encourage and stimulate early language development. It provides a range of ideas for working with young children, most of which require inexpensive equipment and resources such as may be readily available in the home, in the nursery, or in the classroom.

The first part of the book, Introduction, includes suggestions for observing and recording young children's pre-language and language development. The practically based sections of the book cover four main areas: The Foundations of Language; Language Skills; Using Language; Language and Thinking.

In the *Introduction* language development charts offer parents and professionals an opportunity to consider in detail the child's level of language functioning. They guide the user to observe in detail, if required, or to continue directly to a later section if the criteria are fulfilled. Areas for observation and recording include: spoken language; using language; understanding language; following commands; imitation of sounds; imitative and make believe play; objects, and gestures.

*The Foundations of Language.* This section is concerned with helping children to understand the world around them, promoting the development of play, encouraging their listening and attention skills, helping them to imitate, and stimulating early sound making.

*Language Skills.* The next section is designed to help develop children's understanding of words, and to stimulate and encourage their use of words, from the one word level to structuring simple sentences.

*Using Language.* This section concentrates on language and interaction: how to develop communication, how to continue development in everyday settings and how to help children play and talk together.

*Language and Thinking.* This more advanced section covers memory games, classification and the use of language for self direction.

This is essentially a practically based book with games and activity suggestions. Once more it is an example of an endorsement of the policy that language is part of everyday life; and that language stimulation must be carried out as far as possible in naturalistic settings – as part of everyday life.

### *Talking Together* by **Rachel Hall**

This is a book of 'shared language activities for adults and young children' and can be used by parents as well as professionals to help encourage language development. It contains games and activities, with suggestions for their use, which help aid concentration and attention, and listening skills. It is divided into sections, and subdivided into themes. Special symbols are used to indicate specific uses of some of the activities, for example with children with hearing difficulties. It is clearly hand written with simple line drawings and consists of individually laminated pages, which are easily removable so that they may be photocopied for repeated use.

It is a practical, basic activities book which may help anyone devise language and pre-language games which may be fun for young children.

# CHAPTER 9

## Encouraging Language Development

Carolyn Bruce

The aim of any language programme, whether informal or published, is to help children attain a more acceptable level of language and communication skills for their age. This chapter will concentrate on encouraging language development more informally, as part of daily routines and in naturalistic settings, as referred to in Chapter 8.

Once children have been identified as having communication difficulties, it is useful to draw up a detailed description of what they can and cannot do in their daily lives. This may be particularly useful in helping to design an 'informal' language programme which may then be used specifically for an individual child. Children's behaviour in nursery or school, their performance in physical and social activities, as well as their school work should all be noted as these will contribute to a clearer picture of their abilities.

Nursery nurses and teachers have a number of important roles to play when faced with children with communication difficulties. They may have identified the problems and collected information on children's behaviour in the classroom. They may be the key people who will put into effect the language programmes, as well as providing a more sensitive environment for encouraging language development. Also, they may be called upon to monitor whether the children are using their new knowledge in the class setting.

How nursery nurses and teachers perform these roles will be influenced by what they consider language is; what they think are the stages of normal language development, and how they think language is acquired. The speech and language therapist will provide direction and support, but nursery nurses and teachers can ensure that children make maximum progress by providing them with the best conditions for encouraging communication whilst they are in their care.

## Activities to encourage language

Each child is unique. Children with a language problem will require programmes tailored to meet their individual difficulties, needs and interests. In addition, they need to experience normal class activities and conversations. It should be possible to combine the two. Language programmes can be supplemented by classroom activities which encourage conversation in the class and develop underlying language skills.

It may be useful and time saving to collect and store in a box activities that have been enjoyed by the children. This may include some commercially available material as well as activities devised by the staff. For example, these could include games that:

- develop a child's knowledge of the world in specific areas such as colours and size;
- help a child to listen to spoken commands;
- help a child to remember spoken commands;
- help a child follow a short story.

The child's particular language ability will influence the choice of activity. The activities could be organised according to level of difficulty. Thus, easier tasks would be introduced first and harder ones presented only when the child had the necessary skills to progress.

For example, when listening to speech sounds it is easier for a child to distinguish between large differences in sounds and words, such as the difference between 'coat' and 'letter', before moving on to the harder task of choosing between words which sound very similar, such as 'coat' and 'goat'.

It is hard to hear the difference between two words which differ in only one sound, these are minimal pairs as referred to in Chapter 4. 'Car and 'tar' are a minimal pair – the two words differ by only one sound.

So, where the two words which the child has to choose between sound completely different, as in 'coat – letter', and the adult says: 'Show me the coat', it is comparatively easy for the child to pick out the word 'coat'. The task is harder if the adult says, 'Show me the coat', and the pair of words that the child has to choose between is 'coat – goat'. If the child cannot pick out the word 'coat' when paired with 'letter' it is unlikely that s/he would be able to pick out the word 'coat' from the pair 'coat – goat'.

Language tasks may be presented in picture, spoken or written form. Sometimes use can be made of books, commercial materials, toys, computer graphics, everyday objects, and even the children themselves, so long as the message is clear and a child's interest is captured.

## Choosing the right level

Some activities are more complex than others, either because a high level of skill is required, or a number of different skills are involved in one activity. For example, if a child is told to, 'Wash the doll's face', this involves at least three different levels. In order to carry out this instruction, the child has to be able to:

1. Listen to the speaker.
2. Identify and remember the words.
3. Carry out the task by picking up the doll and washing its face.

It is important to look carefully at the skills needed by children in an activity such as this. They need to have the skills to achieve each stage of the activity if they are to succeed with the whole task.

Try and write down the different stages of a number of tasks in the classroom, and discuss these with your colleagues. What might appear to be a simple task to an adult may rely on skills which are developed over the years and which are performed almost automatically.

For example, a popular activity when helping children to improve their attention and listening skills, is to match a sound to a picture. A ball may be matched to the sound /b/ and a tap may be matched to the sound /t/. This matching can be done for all the sounds of English. Children may be given several picture cards, for example, of taps and balls. When they hear an adult make a sound such as /b/ or /t/ they are expected to identify an appropriate picture.

This may be an easy task for an adult, although young children will find it more difficult. Adults may approach this task in two ways:

- they may learn by heart the sounds that are associated with each picture;
- they may use their learned ability to separate out the sounds in a word (phonic skills) and work out that the letter being represented by the picture 'tap' /t-a-p/ is 't'.

Young children are less able to do this task than adults, as they have fewer resources available. They are unlikely to have phonic skills, which are associated with reading; also their ability to remember information is limited. Thus the child's failure to perform the task may be due to limited memory, rather than inability to distinguish between sounds.

The number of skills required to complete a task must be considered. For example, children may find it difficult to build something following the teacher's instructions, as they have to divide their attention between the speaker and the task. But it can be achieved. However, children who have poor hand control when asked to follow spoken instructions at the same time as completing a constructional task, will find it even more difficult, as they are less able to give their full attention to the instructions. It may be easier for them if the instructions were split up into small chunks, the first given before they begin to build. Further instructions should be given only when the teacher has the child's full attention.

## Language programmes

Any language programme should include the identification of language areas that need work and the specification of how this work may be fitted into the child's daily routine. Ideally the language areas, and specific items selected within them, should have maximum impact on the child's ability to influence and understand those around them.

For example, in the case of a nonverbal child. Rather than teaching long lists of 'things' or object names (nouns), a smaller selection of these, plus a number of 'event' or 'action' words (verbs), such as 'do; go, make; be' would enable the child to combine two or more words to make simple sentences. For example: 'Mummy go;' 'Need drink;' 'Mummy make drink.'

It is important that the content of the activities and the way they are introduced should be adapted to each child's language level. Language activities should be incorporated into the child's daily school routine. Encouragement of language should not be restricted to set times and set tasks. Although it may be important to set aside special sessions in order to work on some more formalised language programmes, as discussed in Chapter 8, it must be remembered that in order for language work to be beneficial it needs to become part of, and have an effect on, the child's daily life.

There may be some skill areas such as attention, that require specific help and necessitate the child being withdrawn from the classroom.

However, even these skills will need to become part of children's daily experiences if they are to have an influence on their ability to communicate.

## Ways of responding

In addition to the tasks included in any language programmes, children's levels of functioning are affected by the way in which adults respond to and communicate with them. Too often a conversation between a teacher and a child is one-sided, with the more experienced speaker, the teacher, doing all the talking, and even anticipating the child's response.

Listen to a tape of yourself talking to the children in your class, or get a colleague to write down what you say and comment on your efforts. This is a good way to gain insight into the way you talk and listen in a conversation. At first you may be surprised, but it will help provide a starting point for change. It may be hard to alter your style of speaking, but you should be able to improve how well you listen, and should gain better control over your speed of talking.

If time can be found, consistently, for one adult to play with and talk to a child, communication is likely to become more rewarding. This one-to-one communication with the same person will allow the child to gain confidence in communicating. It will provide opportunities for both the adult and child to adapt to one another's behaviour and style of speaking.

When adults are talking to children, especially children with language difficulties, they need to limit what they say, slow their speech down and leave longer than normal pauses between turns so that children have time to understand what has been said, and put together a reply. Verbal children should be seen as equal partners in the conversation. Their utterances are worth listening to and warrant a response.

Adults, the more experienced communicators, may have to start the conversation which will, ideally, arise from an activity or object that holds the attention of both the adult and child. Then, adults will encourage the exchange of ideas by prompting the child to communicate again.

However, the contributions made to the conversation should be balanced, so the child must be encouraged or allowed to take the lead at times. Children need the opportunity to introduce topics for conversation, ask questions and respond to questions, as soon as they are able. Children are less likely to contribute if the adults continually adopt a controlling role and ask a great number of questions. This situation can arise when adults are busy, especially if children appear to offer little, or their contributions are unintelligible. The danger is that instead of conversation there is interrogation, and children offer less and less. As children's language develops and they practise using their new skills it should be easier to have a conversation with them and to see them as equal partners.

It should be remembered that even nonverbal children who have difficulty with words must still be seen as capable of communicating. Responses should be made to any attempts at communication. Gaze direction, hand pointing, body position and occasional vocalisations may be starting points with some children. These cues often are unclear and may be misinterpreted at times, but at least they give some idea of the child's interests and desire to communicate. Adults will need to use nonverbal responses such as gesture and facial expression, to support their speech when responding to such children.

## How to ensure progress

The aim of encouraging language development is to enable children to use their communication skills to have an effect on the environment. For example, if they want a drink they can ask for some juice. Learning lists of words, phrases and sentences may not be helpful as they are unlikely to be used outside the taught situation.

Children acquire language by identifying the rules that operate in their language from the examples presented to them, and from these make their own sentences which can be used in new situations. Children may overuse certain new rules as explained in Chapter 2, but it is important to recognise them as a part of the learning process.

Clear examples and repetition of the same situations increase the likelihood of connections being made between the words and the rules that govern word and sentence structure. Efforts should be made to ensure that these examples fit into the framework of the language which the child has already acquired, so that the link between ideas, words and rules in a sentence is strengthened. For some children progress will be slow even when attempts are made to structure their environment and the language they hear.

If children are to acquire and use language they hear within the class in new situations, then it must reflect the language of their environment. They need to acquire conversational English and not the form found in old-fashioned grammar books. If a child is shown a picture of a woman cooking and is asked, 'What is the woman doing?', then an acceptable response would be, 'Cooking', 'She is cooking' or 'She's cooking'. 'The lady is cooking' is a stilted, formal version of the response.

## Modelling

As explained in Chapter 2, modelling occurs spontaneously with children when they are acquiring language. If a child is having difficulties learning to talk, then this strategy of modelling may be used to improve and extend what the child says. Thus, the listener uses the child's utterance and takes it one stage further, using the same form but adding to its length and complexity. As in the example below:

Child: 'Cat eat.'
Adult: 'The cat is eating.'
Child: 'Cat eating.'
Adult: 'The cat is eating some fish.'

It may be possible to use modelling to create a new sentence while maintaining the topic as in the next example:

Child: 'The man is shopping.'
Adult: 'Yes, he has bought a shirt.'
Child: 'Look, money.'
Adult: 'He will have to give the lady some money for the shirt.'

## Questions to children

Every effort should be made to use language to convey an appropriate message. Too often the questions we direct at the children are **display questions**, where the child knows that the speaker already has the answer.

For example, a mother asking: 'What colour pencil is this?' where the child realises that she knows the answer because she is looking at the pencil. Questions like this should be kept to a minimum. Instead of using such items that both adult and child can see clearly, and asking, 'What colour is it?' it would be more appropriate for the mother to ask the same question when only the child can see the object and she cannot.

Wood, Wood, Griffiths and Howarth, (1990) state that questions by their very nature are controlling and demanding. They found that if questions are asked in the classroom, the children answer the questions, but say little else. The children made more contributions and longer utterances if there were fewer questions in the conversation. Children may be encouraged to make more contributions if the teachers talk about their own experiences and/or comment on what the child has to offer.

However, it is natural to ask questions, and some will be needed to ensure that the conversation is not incomprehensible. Questions are more successful if they relate to the theme or contribution a child has already made. In addition, nonverbal cues must not conflict with the question.

The teacher may use two-choice questions, for example: 'Are you happy or sad today?'; or 'Wh' questions (Where? What? Why? When?) to begin or to help clarify a topic of conversation. 'Wh' questions are unlikely to get an appropriate response without the children understanding the force of the question, and the importance of the particular question word. They will need to understand the concepts of time and place in order to answer questions beginning with 'When', 'What' or 'Where;' and they will need to have a conceptual understanding of cause and effect before they can answer, 'Why?' or 'How?' questions. (See Chapter 2).

## Feedback

In order that children progress, it is necessary for them to know whether they have been successful in their attempts at communication. Children need to know if they have been successful at conveying their message; and if they have understood speech directed at them. Most of the time it is appropriate to tell them so.

The natural way that adult listeners can indicate that they have understood the child is by doing what is asked, or by continuing the conversation by expanding the topic being discussed. If children's messages are incomplete then an incorrect action or reply will let them know this.

Adults may help children to produce a clearer message by stating that their message was unclear, or seeking confirmation by asking them: 'Do you mean X or Y?' It is more difficult to communicate with a child whose speech is unintelligible as guesswork may be needed to aid interpretation.

If children fail to understand what they are being told or asked to do, then the message may need to be restated more simply. Requests may be repeated so that children have a second attempt at understanding what was said, or they may be broken down into simple stages, thereby reducing the length of the instruction which needs to be held and understood at any one time.

As a last resort it may be possible to demonstrate the request. Altering what is said or increasing the amount of information in the instruction is likely to confuse more than assist the child.

## How to monitor progress

Keeping a record of developing skills and monitoring progress is essential to ensure that genuine improvement is being made by the child. This information will help to establish whether easier communication is a result of an improvement in the adult's ability to interpret the child's speech, or whether what the child says, and how s/he says it has altered. These records also should highlight any change, particularly in children with multiple problems or behavioural difficulties, where progress is slow or often not recognised. It is easy to develop set ideas about children and not 'allow' them to change. Thus children who are difficult to manage may remain a problem, even when their behaviour shows positive signs of change. There is always a danger that the child whose improved behaviour goes unrecognised and unrewarded will stop progressing and begin to fulfil people's expectations.

The records can take the form of tape recordings, checklists, or written records of children's understanding and use of language. The method selected will be influenced by the time available to spend on the task. The information collected will enable the nursery nurse or teacher to know whether the language and activities selected for the children are pitched at an appropriate level and whether they are ready to progress to the next goal.

## What language should be encouraged

Children with language problems mainly use language when they need help with 'toileting' or feeding; attempts at giving information and making social contacts are often limited. Opportunities for using language in this way are more likely to occur in situations of significance to the child, such as discussion of current and home events or future outings. The content of the conversations will depend on the child's language skills. The adult will take the lead in putting words to actions, introducing new vocabulary, or increasing the complexity of a child's utterances. Introduction of new materials needs to be controlled, so that there is recognisable order and progress can be noted. In the case of vocabulary building each new word or idea should be introduced separately, and incorporated into the child's existing knowledge of language and the world.

Children with language difficulties may need an environment that is organised and full of opportunities to hear and use language, but non-stop talking to them is not the answer. Children are likely to tire quickly in tasks which require them to use their weaker skills and after a while they may switch off or opt out. With some children it is obvious when this situation arises, as they move away from the speaker, and even put their hands over their ears. Short, regular sessions during which language is specifically encouraged, which build up the child's abilities gradually are more likely to be successful and rewarding to both parties.

## Who should encourage language?

In order to give children the best chance of improving their communication skills we need to consider the social and physical environment, as well as the content of the exchanges. Children with language difficulties are a varied group. Some may be quiet and withdrawn, whilst others are loud and difficult to manage. All are likely to have impaired contact with their environment.

Activities such as *play*, which use the same skills as language, may be delayed. Play provides children with the opportunity to understand their world, to work with others, and to use their language. Children with communication difficulties may have difficulties starting and developing their play, which may be repetitive and solitary. They may stand and watch other children playing together, but lack the skills required to become involved with another child. Limited play and language skills are likely to result in difficulties interacting with other children.

For children with language problems, support and practise of their communication skills is unlikely to be provided by their peer group. Language handicapped children seldom use their language to form social contacts. Furthermore they are less able to have successful and prolonged conversations with their classmates. Even children who do not have communication problems have a great deal of linguistic knowledge to acquire before they are as mature as adults are in their communication. Thus they are unable, and possibly unwilling, to facilitate a child less able than themselves.

Children with language disorders need the encouragement and the skills of the adults around them in order to help them develop their language. Initially the teacher or nursery nurse may interact with the child on his/her own. As confidence and language skills increase, a child may be introduced to one other child, and then into activities with larger groups of children. The adult's role in starting and maintaining the conversation can gradually be withdrawn.

The child with language difficulties needs a great deal of individual attention and will find group situations hardest to handle. Even normal young children find it no easy matter to make themselves understood in a group setting. A question directed at a particular child is likely to be responded to by a number of children in the group.

Groups may be useful for activities where the children respond at the same time, for example singing, or where they are being given instructions or information, such as story telling. Sometimes in a classroom, groups are less suitable for encouraging conversation.

In order to be able to communicate with different people, in different situations, a variety of opportunities is the ideal.

## Where should language be encouraged?

Conversations for young children are likely to revolve around the happenings and social practices of their everyday life. Although it may be necessary sometimes to withdraw children from the classroom for specific language work, wherever and whenever possible language should be encouraged during their class activities. This will ensure that the language used with the children is useful and meaningful.
The environment can be arranged in order to:

- Maximise the child's need to communicate.
  For example a wanted or needed object can be placed in a clear container with a lid which is difficult to remove, so that the child is more likely to request assistance.
- Make the meanings of words more apparent.
  For example, limit the number of options present and act on/do what the child has actually said.

Many different opportunities can be provided to enable the child to discover the meanings of words and use them in conversations. Be aware of the different situations where a word occurs, for example, the word: 'in.' This may appear in different contexts such as: shopping in the basket; washing in the machine, or juice in the cup.

A shared interest is necessary for communication, so the content of the discussion must be mutually agreed upon. Initially this should be directed by the children's interest, by what they are looking at or playing with in the class. McConkey (1987) suggests that an activity selected by the child is more likely to be maintained and, therefore, is the logical focus for conversation.

Different activities will influence the quantity and content of the language produced by the child. Construction tasks are unlikely to provide the opportunities for extended conversations, similarly if the child is running around they will be out of breath and more concerned with action than with words.

Bruner (1980) found that fantasy play in the 'home corner' and play with dolls were more likely to encourage verbal exchanges. His study also found that children said more in these environments when adults were not involved. However, as discussed earlier, language disordered children need the support of an adult in order to initiate and maintain the conversation.

## Conclusion

Children with language problems are best helped by those who are interested and working with them exchanging information and combining expertise. Improvement in the understanding and use of language will be a gradual process which may continue throughout the children's time in school. The speed of change will depend on the severity of the problem, the quality of help children receive, and on their attitude to their difficulties.

Positive improvement in a child's language development will be encouraged by a nursery nurse or teacher who is genuinely interested and is able to spend time with the child. If this interest and enthusiasm can be combined with an understanding of language development and language breakdown, the children in their care have a real chance of making progress and achieving their full potential.

# CHAPTER 10

# *Working with Parents*

## Carol Miller

## Why work with parents?

For some people, working with parents is an obvious and essential part of their everyday activities with young children. For others, it raises questions about why or how it should happen. Many people who work with young children do so because of a strong interest in them. They feel comfortable in their relationships with the children and are often not happy to do this work in the presence of other adults. However, a strong case can be made for involving parents in the work with their children, particularly if the children have problems which have been identified such as speech and language difficulties. Establishments such as nurseries and primary schools can be seen as an important bridge between home life and the larger world of education, and successful transition through these early stages can be of great significance for a whole family. If this is the view, it also follows that staff who work in these settings have a key role to play.

For most children, parents are the main caregivers. They strongly influence the things that happen to young children and provide opportunities which can assist or hinder a child's development. Because they usually spend a great deal of time with their children, most parents are very knowledgeable about them. There is a growing feeling that, where parents and professionals are involved together with a child's development, time can be very well spent.

## Why children attend nurseries

Before looking at specific aspects of parent-professional work, it is useful to consider why children may need pre-school provision such as playgroups and nurseries, and to look at some of the aims of early education.

Some of the reasons will be primarily about the child's needs and others about the needs of the parents. However, it can be argued that children and their parents are so closely linked that the needs of one inevitably affect the needs of the other. For example, a parent may choose to send a child to a playgroup as they consider that their own home cannot offer the variety of play materials and play mates found in a pre-school play group. The needs of the child are concerned with play opportunities. The needs of the parent are concerned with a desire to do their best for the child. The early school years extend this still further, introducing experiences which will form the foundations of so called life-skills. In another example, the social services department may have recommended that a child attend a nursery in a special 'family centre' with the parent because the parent seemed to require help in caring for the child. There can be no doubt that in this case, the child and the parent both need the nursery place. It would be difficult to think of a case where the child's attendance at the nursery could not be seen also to affect the parent, and, therefore, inclusion of the parent in the child's nursery life is justified.

## What do parents need?

Cunningham and Davis (1985) report that many problems arise when professionals try to talk to parents. Parents complain either that they did not get enough information, or that they were given too much. They also say that they did not understand what they were told. There can be several interpretations of these observations, but there can be no doubt that, from the parent's point of view, things are less than satisfactory. Professionals probably have greater opportunities for training and better access to relevant literature than parents and so it can be argued that professionals should take steps to change matters. Above all professionals should respect parents' needs and make every effort to communicate effectively with them. That is, to talk with them and discuss things in ways they can understand.

Most people have had no experience of children with speech and language problems and parents are no exception. Children usually develop their communication skills very well with no obvious help and without special arrangements being made. For parents therefore, it can be extremely confusing and worrying to have a child who does not talk clearly, because that child does not match up with their expectations of what a child should be like. Talking is a very public matter and one which other people notice. Well-meaning friends or relatives may remark on a child's speech if it does not compare well with that of others. It is highly likely that the parents of a child with a speech problem will feel worried and confused. In times of confusion and anxiety, people need to feel that they are understood.

## Professionals' communication skills

Although this book is about children with speech and language problems, it may be helpful here to consider how successfully adults communicate with each other. Working with people is based on relationships with them and effective communication skills are the vehicle of these relationships. Working together with any other person or group will therefore depend on well developed communication skills. Specifically, people who are effective in helping others have been seen to demonstrate the qualities of: **empathy**, **respect** and **genuineness** through their communication skills.

Empathy implies understanding of, or a desire to understand, another person. In effect, it is the ability to 'stand in another person's shoes,' or 'to see the world through another person's eyes.' Respect indicates an acceptance of a person without judgement and a preparedness to work with them. The genuine person is real to another, and does not use a professional facade or rely on technical expertise to impress another person.

These qualities were described by Carl Rogers (1961) with particular reference to counselling and psychotherapy but they equally apply to other helping situations.

Whilst it may seem difficult to change basic personal qualities, there is no doubt that most people can work to develop skills which convey empathy, respect and genuineness to other people. Staff who wish to include parents in work with children may need to consider how their own communication skills can be enhanced before attempting to help the children.

## Developing effective communication

There are many manuals of communication skills training and it is not intended to provide a full course in this chapter. A few points only will be made and further information can be found in the references provided. It is vital that all professionals who attempt to work with young children should be aware of the specific nature of communication between adults and between children and adults.

Listening and responding are fundamental to successful communication. Evidence that another person is listening can be both verbal and nonverbal and can often encourage another person to talk. This applies equally to adults and to children.

### Listening

Brumfitt (1986) described the features of a good listener:

- does not interrupt;
- does not appear to be judgemental about a person's problems;
- is accepting of what the person says;
- does not undervalue the person's problem by describing an event of worse proportions;
- makes it clear that there is time for the person to talk;
- avoids direct giving of advice;
- attempts to clarify what is obscure;
- gives the speaker full attention.

Practice may be needed to ensure that each of the above points applies in any situation.

### Questioning

Questioning may be essential in order to obtain information or to clarify points. Two types of questions may be used – **closed** and **open**. In closed questions, a specific, generally brief, answer is required. As for example in, 'Are you cold?' or, 'How many children have you?' Open questions allow more, and less predictable, information to be given. For example the following open questions might be asked, 'How does your child respond to new situations?' or, 'How did that make you feel?' It can be seen that open questions allow more opportunity for a variety of information to be given and that the questioner does not necessarily remain in control of the type of information provided.

### Encouraging

Encouraging the other person to continue talking may be important if a parent and professional are to develop a relationship. Sometimes simple encouragements of a nonverbal nature can be given, such as a head nod or just remaining silent. Or encouragements such as, 'Go on', or just saying 'mmm', may help.

### Reflecting

A technique which can be effective is known as 'reflecting': as one person repeats back what the other has just said. For example:

> Parent:   'Sarah's been really terrible this week.'
> Teacher: 'Terrible?'

The teacher's response indicates that the comment has been heard, and the questioning intonation encourages the parent to continue on the same theme. It may help a person to focus on something which they have said without too much forethought. Practice may be required to use this well, as over-use can become particularly ineffective and even irritating.

Within each of these skills outlined above there will be many smaller communication skills. The effective communicator is also aware of the changes in communication which can be made through intonation, variations in loudness, quality of voice, choice of words, and the length of sentences used. The more consciously a person can control these elements of their communication, the more they can be used as tools to create and develop effective working relationships with parents.

## Different ways of working

Because different professional groups often have specific ways of working, it may be difficult to imagine how parents could be involved with activities with their child. It is important to be conscious of the view we have of ourselves as professionals and to see how this affects our particular style of working. For example, we may believe that our training provides us with a very specialised area of knowledge and skills which no other group could adopt. To a certain extent, this is true of every professional group and, in a way, defines 'professional'. However, there are great advantages in sharing skills and knowledge which can enhance rather than diminish effectiveness.

Cunningham and Davis (1985) describe three different frameworks or models which may be used when parents and professionals work together. Whilst these are not always completely separate from each other, it can be useful for practitioners to become conscious of their own preferred way of working, either in all cases or with individual cases at different times.

## Expert model

The first approach to parent work is described as the 'expert model'. In this, the professionals view themselves as having total expertise compared with parents. The professional is responsible for what happens to the child and when the parent is involved in helping, this takes place under the instruction of the professional. There are advantages and disadvantages to this approach. It may give the professional confidence as there is no danger that another person's view needs to be incorporated. On the other hand, it may lead to lack of self-confidence in parents as they believe that no one but the professional is capable of helping their child. The parent may become over-dependent on the professional as a consequence.

## Transplant model

In this model the professional believes that parents can be helpful, but that they need training. The professionals therefore teach the parents how to help the child, thus transplanting professional skills into the parents. There is no doubt that this model enables parents and professionals to work together, but this must always be done under the direction of the professional. The decision-making lies with the professionals and there may not be much opportunity for the parents to discuss their own particular needs or indeed to use their own individual style in doing things.

## Consumer model

In this model the parents are viewed as consumers of services with rights of choice and the ability to select what they want. Discussion is required for agreement to be reached between professional and parents about what is best for the child, and indeed for the whole family. The parents need information from the professional in order to make an informed choice. There must be a two-way flow of information and a balanced relationship must develop between the parents and the professionals. Each must believe that the other has something to offer and that they can not proceed successfully without the other.

It is possible to see that each of these ways of working could be useful in different situations and with different people. Individuals vary enormously and will need differing approaches. The particular philosophy of a nursery or school will also influence ways of working, although it is important not to make too many assumptions without considering individual needs. The importance of identifying these models is to become aware of preferred ways of working and why these have been chosen. Before deciding on what can be done to help a particular child and the family, the professional must consider their own and that family's individual characteristics and consider what might be a suitable approach for all concerned.

It is clear that an evaluation of one's 'working model' cannot be made without a professional being very conscious of their own characteristics and style and knowing a good deal about a particular family. It will also require evaluation of the whole setting in which they are working. This in itself may require new approaches to day to day issues.

## Where to work

The idea of working with parents may necessitate some physical changes. In an extreme example, for instance, it would be difficult to work with parents if they were never allowed through the door of the school or nursery or if they were only allowed in at specific and limited times. Similarly, if information is needed about a child in the context of the family, this may not be available if staff never meet the child outside the work place. Children, like adults, often feel and act quite differently in their own home and it would therefore be important to try to understand this. The environment of a child's home might be very different from a nursery or school, for example in terms of its safety and the facilities available. It would be very useful to be aware of these things and this would necessitate visits to children's homes. Some re-evaluation of arrangements may be necessary if parents and professionals are to meet comfortably in order to develop a working relationship.

## What can be done together?

If we consider the child with speech and language problems, the main concerns will be first, to understand, in as much detail as possible, the difficulties in communicating with the child; and second, to try to resolve them.

### Understanding the child's difficulties

Before drawing up any plans for helping a child, it is essential to describe the child's difficulties (see Chapter 4) and, if possible, to identify what has caused the difficulties or is maintaining them. Assessment forms part of this process. Where the assessment of a child's communication problem is concerned, this needs to consider the child's abilities in several contexts. Some children are assertive at home but say little at nursery or in other people's houses. Communication skills can vary with the topic of conversation and with different conversational partners. When trying to evaluate a child's strengths and weaknesses, note should always be taken of when, where and with whom the activities took place.

Parents are, in most cases, the key source of information about their child. Indeed, where the child in question is at the pre-school level, a case can be made for always including the parents in the assessment.

Dewart and Summers (1995) have developed the Pragmatics Profile of Everyday Communication Skills in Children. Originally, designed for use with very young children, the Profile has now been extended to children up to approximately the age of ten. This schedule for an informal interview with the parent of a young child stresses the importance of parents in the assessment of children's communication. It can be used by anyone who has a professional interest in the development of language and communication and the process of completing the profile enhances awareness of the child's abilities.

Briefly, the Profile consists of a series of questions which are used to promote discussion of the different ways in which a child communicates.

There are no right or wrong answers and no 'score' or 'level of achievement' results. The aim is to discover how a child communicates, rather than what can or cannot be done.

The discussion focuses on four main areas:

1. *Communicative Functions:* What sort of thing the child tries to say, and how. For example, whether gesture is the main form, or whether words are used. How the child asks for things and what they ask for.

2. *Response to Communication:* How the child responds to other people's communications. In this section, it is important to discover whether the child is interested in communication; whether they are aware of the

way people talk, and how they respond to different types of requests and questions.

3. *Interaction and Communication:* This section looks at how exchanges in communication take place. Children vary in the amount of interest show in communication and the section explores whether communications are mainly verbal or nonverbal.

4. *Contextual Variation:* This deals with changes in the child's communication according to the time, topic, place and partner.

The questions used in the Profile invite the persons being interviewed to provide recent examples of the child's communications and it is clear that the process of going through the interview can, in itself, be a learning experience for those concerned. Having to tell someone about their child can make parents more aware of particular details. It may draw attention to areas which the parent has never thought of and which they may then go away and observe more carefully.

The completion of the Pragmatics Profile of Everyday Communication Skills in Children is, by its nature, a collaborative activity between a parent and a professional. This author used it as the main tool of assessment of children's communication in a Social Services' family centre. Parents who were mainly living in extremely deprived social circumstances and who were often preoccupied with fundamental environmental needs, proved to be good observers of their children. They were keen and pleased to talk about their children and there was evidence that taking part in the interview raised their awareness of their children's communication. Following completion of the Profile, they would frequently volunteer further details and examples in later weeks as they appeared to realised what was of interest.

Assessment of a child's communication skills can, in some instances, be a formal affair which can mystify parents and occasionally cause them anxiety. An assessment in which they are involved and over which they have considerable control can be of enormous practical use. In addition, the nature of an informal interview can itself enhance the relationship between parent and professional and provide a parent with indications that the professional is interested in them and their child. It may, of course, be necessary for a child to be seen for more specific investigations and for parents to be asked very particular questions which may help professionals to identify the possible causes of difficulties. A positive relationship with the parents will facilitate the process of investigation and assessment.

### *Helping the child and the parents*

A description of a child's communication will assist in identifying where help may be needed. Like other aspects of a child's development, speech and language are not confined to specific times of the day or to particular places. Neither are they the property of specialists or individual professionals. Communication skills are used by everyone and, in the case of children, a variety of people will contribute to their development.

Parents are generally keen to be involved with their children but it is important to remember that they are parents and not teachers or therapists. For this reason, professionals who choose to work with parents need to be mindful of the very particular nature of parent-child relationships. Cunningham and Davis (1985) discuss five factors which relate to parenting and which affect the child's well-being.

1. The quality of the physical environment.
2. The expression of warmth and affection towards the child.
3. Sensitivity to the child's needs as reflected in the quality of interactions.
4. The use of control over the child's actions.
5. Active involvement with the child.

When working with parents to help a child's speech and language development, it can be helpful to keep these factors in mind and allow them to influence communications with parents.

1. The physical environment, that is, the child's surroundings, provides opportunities to play and explore. The nature of this environment can be discussed with parents and suggestions can be made about how the environment might be used. Such discussion presupposes that the parent and the professional are familiar with each other's environment so that unrealistic ideas are not explored. It is important to know the possible limitations of what a parent can provide and how the nursery or school and the home can complement each other. Opportunities to observe in the nursery or school may present parents with examples of activities which they can adopt or adapt for home use.

2. The child's confidence and self-esteem will develop from the expression of warmth and affection coming from others. For most children, these come first and foremost from their family. There is a danger that the child with a speech and language difficulty, or other problem, may be viewed less positively than others and it may be very important for parents to become aware of positive aspects of their

child. Occasionally some **reframing** may be helpful. For example, when a parent is concerned their child 'can't talk' it may be helpful to point out that nevertheless the child 'communicates', very well as many children understand others and use gesture and meaningful noises very effectively. The same issue can then be seen from a different point of view. The school or nursery may also provide parents with an opportunity to see their child doing new things which they have not witnessed before.

3. Being responsive to a child is a key process in the development of communication. Anxious parents (and professionals) are often seen to be trying to 'make' a child talk by demanding, 'Say this,' or asking, 'What's that?' Such parents may themselves require sensitive responses and may need to be helped to listen and respond more to their child's communicative attempts. As people listen and make efforts to understand, a child begins to realise the value of communication and is likely to make further attempts.

4. Cunningham and Davis observe that children are often less compliant with their parents than with teachers. They believe that the freedom or amount of control given by parents may be important for a child to explore the limits of what is permitted and the particular rules within the special relationship. Professionals need to be conscious of the differences in children's behaviour in different situations. Parents may become embarrassed and anxious if their child 'misbehaves' in front of a teacher or therapist or may lose confidence if a professional appears to 'handle' their child better than they do. They may be upset if they consider their child as 'difficult' or a 'problem' and this is not borne out by the child's performance with staff. It is important for parents and professionals to discuss this and to agree on mutually acceptable ways of working.

5. Active involvement or engagement with a child is highly desirable for the development of speech and language. In the same way that parents and professionals are to be encouraged to share skills and ideas, exchanges between adults and children will promote the development of speech and language. Where specific 'techniques' are suggested to assist particular aspects of speech, care must be taken that these are not carried out over-zealously at the expense of relaxed games and activities. Excessive focus on speech may lead to self-consciousness on the part of the child and to anxiety in the parents.

There can be no rules for working with parents. The experience will vary in every case. Perhaps it is most successful when professionals are conscious of their own skills and knowledge and of the limitations of these. All of the guidelines given above apply equally to relationships between professionals as well as to those with parents. In selecting the models of working and the communication skills to be used, there may be some value in first discussing and clarifying these with professionals and colleagues. When these are clear, efforts can be made to develop productive working relationships with parents.

# Glossary

BLISSYMBOLICS: Charles Bliss devised a structured code of diagrammatic symbols to represent spoken words. They must be accurately drawn with a template. Used most widely with physically handicapped people to help them communicate.

BRITISH SIGN LANGUAGE (BSL): The sign language used by most deaf people in Britain. It does not follow the same word order as spoken English, but has a grammar and structure of its own.

CEREBRAL PALSY: Brain damage which may occur before, during or shortly after birth. Children with cerebral palsy usually have some degree of physical handicap, which may affect communication. In some cases children may also be intellectually impaired (see Learning Disabilities).

CHILD DIRECTED SPEECH (MOTHERESE): The simplified speech and language patterns which are spontaneously used by adults and older children when talking to young children. It includes the simplification of syntax, the use shorter sentences and the characteristic 'sing-song' intonation pattern which is automatically used.

CLEFT PALATE: A structural abnormality which affects the developing foetus and is present at birth. It involves the two halves of the hard palate and/or soft palate (roof of the mouth) which fail to meet completely. It is often associated with a hare lip. Both conditions are normally treatable surgically. There may be feeding difficulties, and some articulation problems may occur.

CONDUCTIVE HEARING LOSS: A hearing impairment caused by damage to the outer or middle ear.

ENGLISH AS A SECOND LANGUAGE (ESL or E2L): Refers to children for whom English is not the language spoken in the home. They learn, and often use, English as their second language.

MILD/MODERATE/SEVERE LEARNING DISABILITIES: Refers to people who have some degree of intellectual impairment. Previously referred to as, 'Mental Handicap'.

MAKATON: Over 300 specific signs which have been specially selected from BSL. The key words in spoken sentences are signed. It is widely used with people with learning disabilities to help them communicate.

MAKATON SYMBOLS: A system of stylised pictures which are used to represent the signs of MAKATON. (See REBUS). They may be hand drawn. Often used in conjunction with MAKATON (see above) to aid communication.

OTITIS MEDIA: An inflammation in the middle ear.

PAGET GORMAN SIGNED SPEECH (PGSS): The first sign language system, devised for deaf people, to follow the same word order and grammatical patterns as spoken English. It is used as a language teaching tool with children with specific speech and language disorders.

REBUS: A system of stylised pictures which are used as symbols to represent words. Some may look like the words which they represent, such as 'ball'; some are easy to guess, such as the 'plus' symbol meaning 'and'; others are more arbitrary such as those which represent 'in' and 'on'. They are used to help children with communication problems to communicate, and as an introduction to reading.

SENSORI-NEURAL HEARING LOSS: A hearing impairment caused by a lesion in the cochlea or in the cochlear branch of the VIIIth cranial nerve.

# References and Further Reading

Adams, M.R. (1977) A clinical strategy for differentiating the normal nonfluent child and the incipient stutterer *Journal of Fluency Disorders* **2** pp.141–148.

Andrews, G. and Harris, M. (1964) *The Syndrome of Stuttering London*. The Spastics Society with W. Heinemann Medical Books.

Association for All Speech Impaired Children (AFASIC) (1989) *Breaking Down the Communication Barrier*. London: AFASIC.

Bishop, D.V.M. and Edmundson, A. (1986) 'Is otitis media a major cause of specific developmental language disorder?' *British Journal of Disorders of Communication*, Vol. 121, No. 3, pp.321–338.

Bloodstein, O. (1981) *A Handbook on Stuttering*. Chicago, USA: National Easter Seal Society.

Brumfitt, S. (1986) *Counselling*. Bicester: Winslow Press.

Bruner, J. (1980) *Under Five in Britain*. Oxford Preschool Research Project: Grant McIntyre Ltd.

Bruner, J.S. (1975) 'The Ontogenesis of Speech Acts'. *Journal of Child Language*, Vol. 2, No. 1, pp.1–20.

Chomsky, C. (1969) *The Acquisition of Syntax in Children of 5–10*. Research Monograph 57: MIT Press.

Chomsky, N.A. (1959) Review of *Verbal Behaviour* by B. F. Skinner, **Language 35.** pp.26–58.

College of Speech and Language Therapists (1991) *Communicating Quality*, London: CSLT.

Conture, E.G and Caruso, A.J. (1987) 'Assessment and Diagnosis of Childhood Dysfluency' in L. Rustin; H. Purser and D. Rowley (Eds) *Progress in the Treatment of Fluency Disorders*. London: Taylor and Francis.

Cooke, J. and Williams, D. (1985) *Working with Children's Language*. Bicester: Winslow Press.

Cooper, E.B. and Cooper C.S. (1985) *Personalised Fluency Control Therapy*, Revised. Allen, TX: DLM Teaching Resources.

Coupe, J. and Goldbart, J. (Eds) (1988) *Communication Before Speech: Normal Development and Impaired Communication*. London: Croom Helm.

Crystal, D. (1984) *Language Handicap in Children*. Oxford: National Council for Special Education.

Crystal, D. (1986) *Listen to your Child: Parent's Guide to Children's Language*. Harmondsworth: Penguin Books.

Cunningham, C. and Davis, H. (1985) *Working with Parents: Frameworks for Collaboration*. Milton Keynes: Open University.

Davis, A. (1993) 'A public health perspective on childhood hearing impairment' in B McCormick (Ed) *Paediatric Audiology 0–5 years* (2nd Ed). London: Whurr Publishers.

Dewart, H. and Summers, S. (1995) *The Pragmatics Profile of Everyday Communication Skills in Children*. Windsor: NFER-Nelson.

Fryer, A. (1994) 'The Hanen Early Language Parent Programme' in J. Law (Ed) *Before School: A Handbook of Approaches to Intervention with Pre-School Language Impaired Children*. London: AFASIC.

Gibbin, K.P. (1993) 'Otological considerations in the first 5 years of life' in B McCormick (Ed) *Paediatric Audiology 0–5 years* (2nd Ed). London: Whurr Publishers.

Gregory, H.H. and Hill, D. (1980) 'Stuttering Therapy for Children in W.H. Perkins (Ed.) *Strategies in Stuttering Therapy*. New York: Thieme-Stratton.

Haggard, M.P., Birkin, J.A. and Pringle, D.P. (1993) 'Consequences of otitis media for speech and language' in B McCormick (Ed) *Paediatric Audiology 0–5 years* (2nd Ed). London: Whurr Publishers.

Haggard, M.P. and Hughes, E. (1991) *Screening children's hearing: a review of the literature and the implications of otitis media*. London: HMSO.

Hall, D.M.B., Hill, P. and Elliman, D. (1990) *The Child Surveillance Handbook*. Oxford: Radcliffe Medical Press.

Hall, R. (1990) *Talking Together*. Northumberland: STASS Publications.

Harris, J. (1990) *Early Language Development*. London: Routledge.

Harris, J. (1984) 'Early Language Intervention Programmes: An Update' *Association of Child Psychology and Psychiatry* Vol. 6 No. 2, pp.2–20

Herbert, M. (1987) *Behavioural Treatment of Children's Problems*. London: Academic Press.

Jeffrie, D. and McConkey, R. (1976) *Let Me Speak*. Souvenir Press Educational and Academic Ltd.

Kelman, E. and Schneider, C. (1994) 'Parent-Child Interaction: An Alternative Approach to the Management of Children's Language Difficulties', *Child Language Teaching and Therapy*, Vol. 10, No. 1 pp.81–96.

Kidd, K.K., Kidd, J.R. and Records, M.A. (1978) 'The Possible Causes of the Sex Ratio in Stuttering and its Implications', *Journal of Fluency Disorders*, 3, pp.13-23.

Knowles, W. and Masidlover, M. (1982) *The Derbyshire Language Scheme*. Derbyshire Education Authority.

Law, J. (Ed) (1992) *The Early Identification of Language Impairment in Children*. London: Chapman and Hall.

Locke, A. (1994) Classroom Approaches in J. Law (Ed) *Before School: A Handbook of Approaches to Intervention with Pre-School Language Impaired Children.* London: AFASIC.

Locke, A. (1985) *Living Language*. Windsor: NFER Nelson.

Locke, A. and Beech, M. (1991) *Teaching Talking*. Windsor: NFER Nelson.

McConkey, R. and Price, P. (1986) *Let's Talk: Learning Language in Everyday Settings*. London: Souvenir Press.

McConkey, R. and Gallagher, F (1984) *Let's Play*. London Souvenir Press.

McCormick, B. (1993) 'Behavioural hearing tests 6 months to 3:6 years' in B. McCormick (Ed) *Paediatric Audiology 0–5 years* (2nd Ed). London: Whurr Publishers.

Masidlover, M. (1994) 'The Derbyshire Language Scheme' in J. Law (Ed) *Before School: A Handbook of Approaches to Intervention with Pre-School Language Impaired Children*. London: AFASIC.

Meyers, S.C. and Woodford, L.L. (1992) *The Fluency Development System*. Buffalo New York: United Educational Services.

Miller, C. (1991) 'The Needs of Teachers with Children with Speech and Language Disorders', *Child Language Teaching and Therapy* Vol. 7, No. 2, pp.179–191.

MorganBarry, R.A. (1988) *Auditory Discrimination and Attention Test*. Windsor: NFER-Nelson.

Murray, H.L. and Reed, C.G. (1977) 'Language Abilities of Pre-school Stuttering Children' *Journal of Fluency Disorders* 2, pp.171–176.

Newark, T. (1984) *Not Good at Talking*. Bath: Barton Books.

Prizant, B.M., Audet, L.R., Burke, G.M., Hummel, L.J., Maher, S.R. and Theadore, G. (1990) 'Communication Disorders and Emotional/Behavioural Disorders in Children and Adolescents' *Journal of Speech and Hearing Disorders*, **55**, pp.179–192.

Richman, N., Stevenson, J. and Graham, P. (1982) *Pre-school to school: a behavioural study*. London: Academic Press.

Riley, G. (1980) *Stuttering Severity Instrument for Children and Adults*. Revised Edition. Oregon, USA: C.C. Publications.

Riley, G.D. and Riley, J.A. (1984) 'A component model for treating stuttering in children' in M. Peins (Ed) *Contemporary Approaches in Stuttering Therapy*. Boston, USA: Little, Brown & Co.

Rogers, C. (1961) *On Becoming a Person*. London: Constable.

Rutter, M., Cox, A., Tupling, C., Berger, M. and Yule, W. (1975) 'Attainment and Adjustment in Two Geographical Areas: Prevalence of Psychiatric Disorders' *British Journal of Psychiatry*, **126**, pp.493–509.

Sheehan, J.G. (1970) (Ed) *Stuttering Research and Therapy*. New York: Harper and Row.

Snowling, M. (1987) *Dyslexia: a Cognitive Developmental Perspective*. Oxford: Blackwell.

Syder, D. (1992) *An Introduction to Communication Disorders*. London: Chapman and Hall.

Tucker, I. and Nolan, M. (1984) *Educational Audiology*. London: Croom Helm.

Van Riper, C. (1982) (2nd Edition) *The Nature of Stuttering*. New Jersey, USA: Prentice-Hall.

VOCAL (Voluntary Organisations Communication and Language) (1987) *A Survey of Speech Therapy Services for Children with Particular Reference to Special Education*. London: VOCAL.

Walle, E. (1976) *The Prevention of Stuttering* (Film) Memphis: Speech Foundation of America.

Webster, A. (1988) 'The Prevalence of Speech and Language Difficulties in Childhood: some brief research notes'. *Child Language Teaching and Therapy*, Vol 4, No. 1, pp.85–91.

Webster, A. (1986) *Deafness, development and literacy*. London: Methuen.

Weiss, C.E., and Lilleywhite, H.S. (1981) (2nd Edition) *Communicative Disorders*. St Louis: The CV Mosby Co.

Weiss, C.E.; Lilleywhite, H.S. and Gordon, M.E. (1980) *Clinical Management of Articulation Disorders*. St Louis: The CV Mosby Co.

Weitzman, E. (1992) *Learning Language and Loving It*. Toronto: Hanen Centre.

Wood, D., Wood, H., Griffiths, A. and Hawarth, I. (1990) *Teaching and Talking with Deaf Children*. Chichester: John Wiley & Sons.

# *Further Reading*

Byrne, R. (1991) (Revised Edition) *Let's Talk about Stammering*. London: Association for Stammerers.

Irwin, A. (1988) *Stammering in Young Children*. Wellingborough: Thorsons Publishing Ltd.

Robinson, K. (1991) *Children of Silence*. Harmondsworth: Penguin.

Shaw, C. (1995) *Talking and Your Child*. Hodder and Stoughton.

Wolff, S. (1981) (Second Edition) *Children under Stress*. Harmondsworth: Pelican Books.

# Appendix
## Useful Addresses

**AFASIC**
Association for All Speech
Impaired Children
347 Central Markets
Smithfield
London, EC1A 9NH

**Blissymbols**
Blissymbolics Resource Centre
UK
Thomas House
South Glamorgan Institute for Higher
Education
Cymcoed Centre Cyncoed Rd
Cardiff CF2 6YD

**The British Stammering
Association**
St Margaret's House
21 Old Ford Road
Bethnal Green
London E2 9PL
(If writing please enclose s.a.e.)

**British Sign Language**
The Royal National Institute for
the Deaf
105 Gower St
London WC1E 6AH

(For **Derbyshire Language Scheme**)
Mark Masidlover
Chief Educational Psychologist
Derbyshire Education Authority
Grosvenor Rd
Ripley DE5 3JE

**The Hanen Centre**
252 Bloor St West
Suite 3–390
Toronto
M5S 1VS
Canada

**Lynne Houseman
Hanen Instructor**
and Representative for UK/Ireland
8 Campion Close
Ecceshall
Staffordshire ST21 6SR

**Makaton + Makaton Symbols**
Makaton Vocabulary
Development Project
The Director
31 Firwood Drive
Camberley, Surrey

**Paget Gorman Sign System**
3 Gypsy Lane
Headington
Oxfordshire

# Index